Savages
and Naturals

Savages
and Naturals

Black Portraits by White Writers
in Modern American Literature

John R. Cooley

Newark
University of Delaware Press
London and Toronto: Associated University Presses

©1982 by Associated University Presses, Inc.

Associated University Presses, Inc.
4 Cornwall Drive
East Brunswick,
New Jersey 08816

Associated University Presses
69 Fleet Street
London EC4Y 1EU, England

Associated University Presses
Toronto M5E 1A7, Canada

Library of Congress Cataloging in Publication Data
Cooley, John R   1937-
   Savages and naturals.

   Bibliography: p.
   Includes index.
   1. American literature-20th century-History and criticism.
   2. Afro-Americans in literature.
   3. Primitivism in literature. I. Title.
PS173.N4C6   810'.9'352   79-19288
ISBN 0-87413-167-7

Printed in the United States of America

For Sidney Kaplan

Contents

Preface

In *Invisible Man* Ralph Ellison's protagonist meets a white woman who invites him to her apartment after a speech he has just given on "The Woman Question." The conversation begins:

"...I suppose that's why I always thrill to hear you speak, somehow you convey the great throbbing vitality of the movement. It's really amazing. You give me such a feeling of security — although," she interrupted herself with a mysterious smile, "I must confess that you also make me afraid."

"Afraid? You can't mean that," I said.

"Really," she repeated, as I laughed. "It's so powerful, so — so *primitive.*"

I felt some of the air escape from the room, leaving it unnaturally quiet. "You don't mean primitive?" I said.

"Yes, *primitive*; no one has told you, Brother, that at times you have tom-toms beating in your voice?"

"My God," I laughed, "I thought that was the beat of profound ideas."[1]

The promiscuous attribution of "primitivism" to black character is one form of imposing character invisibility; it places a mask over a real face. The conversation above develops its explosive irony from the contrast between a primitivism the white woman imagines she sees and the desperate attempts of Ellison's black hero to be seen as an

9

individual. As this scene implies, primitivism resides in the eye and mind of the beholder and not in the object, whether a particular person, a landscape, or a way of life. It springs into existence whenever a certain kind of observer calls it forth.

In his autobiography *The Big Sea*, Langston Hughes comments on the primitivism demanded of him by a white patroness during his early years as a writer in Harlem:

> She wanted me to be primitive and know and feel the intuitions of the primitive. But, unfortunately, I did not feel the rhythms of the primitive surging through me, and so I could not live and write as though I did. I was only an American Negro — who had loved the surface of Africa and the rhythms of Africa — but I was not Africa. I was Chicago and Kansas City and Broadway and Harlem. And I was not what she wanted me to be.[2]

Hughes's patroness also wanted him to find a black composer and produce an opera embodying certain images of blackness pleasing to her. Eventually he severed the relationship: the white woman's demands were "like a trap closing in . . . ."[3] She was a threat to both his art and his self-identity.

These two incidents represent a quality of racial perception blacks have known about for a long time — the tendency in the white imagination and in its literature to thrust into black character aspects of the idea of the primitive. The intention of this book is to illustrate the two principal forms this idea assumes in white handling of black characters.[4]

A surprising number of white literary portraits of black Americans are heavily influenced by aspects of primitivism. This compulsion among white writers to primitivize blacks is neither a purely American nor a distinctively twentieth-century tendency, although this study will emphasize the literature of modern America.

The difficulty encountered in discussions of primitivism

stems in part from semantic confusion, for the term is used in different contexts to refer to several very different ideas. For instance, "primitive" is used by the observer of landscape to designate that zone of nature that stretches away from the city, beyond farm and pasture, to the wilderness or jungle. But "primitive" is also value judgment. It is a designation of contrast made by one who sees himself as civilized and wishes to call attention to "uncivilized" people, life-styles, or landscapes. The purpose of the contrast may be either to elevate or to denigrate the "primitive," depending entirely upon the concept of nature, of man, of race, and of civilization held by the observer. One observer, for example, may consider uncivilized land inherently evil. Another may consider the city evil, deminishing man from his formerly elevated state of grace in nature. Yet both may designate man in nature as "primitive." The terms *savage* and *noble savage* reflect this contrariety of attitude.

Although important distinctions can be made between agricultural and wilderness landscapes, "the primitive," as a literary concept, embraces any people and landscapes an author or character in a given work considers to be primitive. Thus, primitivism, as a viewpoint of the appraiser, may seem to exist in the metropolis as well as the wilderness. A musician, bus driver, or politician may be called primitive as easily as a farmer, hunter, or trapper.

Unfortunately, very few works have attempted to challenge and clarify thinking about primitivism. Many literary critics have assumed that primitivist works are basically alike. Under the designation "the primitive of the 1920's," Frederick Hoffman, for example, throws together Sherwood Anderson's *Dark Laughter,* Eugene O'Neill's *The Emperor Jones,* Waldo Frank's *Holiday,* and Carl Van Vechten's *Nigger Heaven,* seeing them all as reactions to "the standardization caused by a modern science in all its social applications."[5] Robert Bone makes a similar generalization in *The Negro Novel in America,* disposing of O'Neill, Frank, Anderson,

DuBose Heyward (*Porgy* and *Mamba's Daughter*) and Van Vechten as exploiters of the common ground of primitivism.[6] The intention here is to discriminate among primitivisms, and in so doing indicate how contradictory they are.

This study is an exploration of types: the works discussed will be placed in one of two modes of primitivism that are designated "the savage" and "the natural." Central to the savage mode is a belief that wild, unaxed nature is evil, and that those who live or have lived in it are a fallen, primitive people, who represent a threat both to Christianity and to civilized society. As Roy Harvey Pearce makes clear, long after the Indian had been subdued, white America continued to search for vestiges of the savage, reviving its "search and destroy" fantasy again and again.[7]

By contrast, the literature of the natural mode expresses a belief that nature is good — a belief always rooted in a general apprehension of civilization. Symptomatic of the mode is a notion that the times (regardless of when) are all wrong because of the unnatural complexity of "modern life." At its heart is a search for images of the "natural man" and a conviction that in nature are to be found models for the restoration of that which is "normal" to the individual and to society. Writers in the natural mode habitually find their models in children, hunters, farmers, rustics, and the aged. In American literature there is special fondness for Indians and blacks as exemplars of the natural mode.

It would be an oversight not to mention at the outset that it has been extremely difficult for white writers to describe black life, and that the relationship of black and white has been, at the very least, agonizing for many white writers, as for many Americans. The challenge and dilemma of how to portray black life has been considerable for certain white writers.[8] One might speculate, in fact, that the higher the level of realistic awareness of black life, the more difficult the writing of such portraits has become.

This work will attempt to determine the degree to which

primitivistic portraits enhance or inhibit good writing and good characterizations. It will also comment on the few occasions when white writers have broken through the facile masks of the primitive to produce portraits of black individuals who reveal something of the special texture and complexity of their lives. The intention, however, is not to provide an exhaustive and broad-brush survey of works that primitivize black character. The subject is better served by selective focus and detailed commentary on nine authors notable for their literary prominence and the significance of their work. These discussions should make clear the central features of these two modes of primitivism, the savage, and the natural. They should also suggest a method for approaching other primitive portraits that do not receive critical comment herein.

Superior writers almost always rise above propaganda and cliché. Their portraits, even of minor figures, stretch toward the revelation of character uniqueness. Successful characters are fictional human beings; they contain a reality and a presence of their own. Nearly all theories of language and fiction demand characters who emerge from their pages to exist independently of their creators. Obviously, shadows, scarecrows, and phantoms cannot do this. Writers approach real achievement when they discover how to breathe life into their characters, even characters of different race, sex and circumstance. Readers have to be given the verbal texture of a character's world if such a person is to become renewably fascinating. When an author captures the language of a character and creates the verbal space he or she inhabits, one begins to see and feel the world in an altered way.

As will become quickly apparent in this book, any intellectual preconception of a character's essential nature severely handicaps a writer. As William Gass expresses it, "Characters are like primary substances . . .great character is the single most obvious mark of great literature."[9] Writing from a program or intellectual conception seldom results in great character. Thrusting black character into primitive form is an example of this kind of barrier to the creation of fictional human beings. There are some very understandable reasons for the tendency to primitivism, but it hinders enormously the process of fiction. On rare occasion white writers, while still attracted to the primitive, have broken through to create black characters who come very close to living purely in and for themselves.

Acknowledgments

Since no book is the product of a single mind, I must mention a few of the many people to whom I am indebted for their contributions to this volume: the late Professor Donald Dike of Syracuse, who taught me so much about fiction and expecially about William Faulkner; Professors Doris Abramson and Jules Chametzky of The University of Massachusetts, who critiqued the manuscript in its early stages; Professors Victor Kramer and Robert Stallman for their suggestions and encouragement; Professor Marcus Cunliffe, who raised some fascinating questions and provided support through a Visiting Research Fellowship at the University of Sussex.

I believe it accurate to say that without the generous support of Western Michigan University, this book would not have been completed. The University provided a sustaining sabbatical leave and a faculty research fellowship; its English department provided the much-needed clerical assistance.

I would like to thank the following for permission to quote from published or unpublished works:

Ball State University Forum for "Blacks as Primitives in Eudora Welty's Fiction" by John R. Cooley, vol. 14, no. 3, pp. 20-28, ©1973 by Ball State University Forum.

Markham Review for " 'The Monster'—Stephen Crane's 'Invisible Man' " by John R. Cooley, vol. 5, pp. 10-14, ©1975 by Wagner College.

G. P. Putnam's Sons for "The White Negro" from *Advertisements for Myself* by Norman Mailer, ©1960 by G. P. Putnam's Sons.

Studies in the Literary Imagination for "*The Emperor Jones and the Harlem Renaissance*" by John R. Cooley, vol. 7, no. 2, pp. 73-83, ©1974 by the Department of English, Georgia State University.

Kurt Vonnegut, Jr., for the letter to John Cooley, June 28, 1975.

My greatest debt and fullest appreciation go to Professor Sidney Kaplan, also of Massachusetts, to whom this work is dedicated. He believed in my project and began to speak of it as a book long before I dared do so. He has witnessed its progress through formative stages and has given abundantly of his intelligence.

Finally, for their patience and understanding, I give heartfelt appreciation to my wife Barbara, my daughters Carolyn and Meredith.

Kalamazoo, Michigan

Savages
and Naturals

1.   Background and Prototypes

The tendency in white American writing to portray blacks as primitives must be viewed both as continuation of the ancient and persistent fascination with primitivisms in the thought and literature of Western civilization and as a product of the peculiarities of the American experience. The contradictory attitudes behind these two styles of expression, the savage and the natural, may be seen, as "puritan" and "Rousseauistic." In the first, the primitive character is seen as evil, as a source of terror, violation, and death, because nature itself is evil. In the second, the primitive character takes on the attributes of the noble savage; he services civilized needs as servant, entertainer, companion, teacher, or savior.

This ambivalence in handling primitives — between the demonic and the angelic, the depraved and the innocent — illuminates, as Leo Marx expresses it, an important aspect of the "moral geography of the American imagination" and its literature.[1] At the start of the age of settlement Elizabethans held these views about the New World. To many Elizabethans America was a place of hellish darkness, filled with cannibalistic and bestial savages. Either God's curse was upon it or it contained all the malevolent forces of the cosmos. William Strachey, arriving off New England in 1609, described what he saw as a "hideous wilderness." His vessels were caught in "a dreadfull storme . . .which swelling, and roaring as it were by fits . . .at length did beate all light from heaven;

which like an hell of darkenesse turned blacke upon us....."[2]
Similarly, William Bradford, in his account of the landing of
the *Mayflower*, saw the Cape Cod shoreline before him as a
"hidious and desolate wilderness, full of wild beasts and wild
men.... The whole countrie, full of woods and thickets,
represented a wild and savage heiw."[3]

To many other Elizabethans the New World seemed quite
the opposite of hideous wilderness. The continent seemed to
them a glimpse of how the world might have looked at
creation. America was the lost Eden, paradise regained.
Captain Arthur Barlowe, dispatched by Sir Walter Raleigh,
tells of his landing on the Virginia coast in just such terms:

> [We] found shole water wher we smelt so sweet, and so
> strong a smel, as if we had bene in the midst of some
> delicate garden abounding with all kinde of odoriferous
> flowers...so full of grapes, as the very beating and surge
> of the Sea overflowed them, of which we found such
> plentie, as well there as in all places else, both on the sand
> and on the greene soile of the hils...and I thinke in all the
> world the like abundance is not to be found.[4]

The idea of America as a garden dominates Captain Barlowe's
report. This garden metaphor, in fact, became a recurrent
image of the New World. Many early reports on the Indians
meshed perfectly with this Arcadian image of primal nature
untouched by history. The pristine earth and its people
stood not just for abundance from nature, but for the
superiority of a simple, rustic way of life. The American
version of cultural primitivism (called the "natural mode"
here) stems from this attitude toward nature and the people
of nature.

Actual conditions in America obviously supported both
sets of images, of the hideous wilderness and the bountiful
garden, of the savage and the natural. These basic metaphors,
of depravity and goodness, found everywhere in the literature
of American settlement and expansion, provide the settings

for numerous relationships of white with non-white Americans — relationships typically presented as either nightmares or dreams. Leslie Fiedler writes,

> It is clear...that deep in the mind of America...there exist side by side a dream and a nightmare of race relations and that the two together constitute a legend of the American frontier, of the West (when the second race is the Indian), or of the South (when the second race is the Negro). In either case, it is the legend of a lost Eden, or in more secular terms, of a decline from a Golden Age to an Age of Iron.... What makes the Golden Age golden, is, in the case of the Indian...an imagined state of peace between white man and red man, transplanted European and aboriginal at home: love, innocence, a kind of religious, even other-worldly calm, preside over the peace. And what makes the Iron Age iron is a state of war between redskin natives and paleface invaders: a burden of hatred and guilt, a history of scalpings and counter-scalpings, revenges and counter-revenges, make this war ultimate hell.[5]

To see in greater detail these alternate legends of the land and of the relationships of white and non-white two centuries after Barlowe and Bradford, one can turn to Henry David Thoreau's *A Week on the Concord and Merrimack Rivers* (1849). In the course of Thoreau's diverse commentary he describes two incidents involving Indians and whites. One of the tales describes the abduction of Hannah Dustan by a band of savages:

> On the 15th of March previous, Hannah Dustan had been compelled to rise from childbed, and half dressed... commence an uncertain march...through the snow and the wilderness. She had seen her seven elder children flee with their father.... She had seen her infant's brains dashed out against an apple-tree.[6]

When she reaches the wigwam of her captors Hannah is told

she and her nurses are "soon to be taken to a distant Indian
settlement, and there made to run the gauntlet naked."
Responding to the threat of further removal, exposure, and
sexual assault, Hannah outwits her captors, killing them in
their sleep. Thoreau describes a terrifying world in which
one must either kill or be killed. At the tale's conclusion,
Mrs. Dustan and her family are happily reunited. Hannah,
incidentally, returns with ten Indian scalps in the bottom of
her canoe, and the General Court pays fifty pounds apiece
for them.[7] Although the primeval forest seems to Mrs.
Dustan and to other settlers "a drear and howling wilderness,"
from his broader view Thoreau makes clear the limitations
of this perspective. The same landscape is "to the Indian a
home, adapted to his nature, and cheerful as the smile of the
Great Spirit.[8]

A tale of much the opposite cast, also from Thoreau's
Week, deals with the idyllic friendship of the fur trader
Alexander Henry and the Indian Wawatam.

> The stern, imperturbable warrior, after fasting, solitude,
> and mortification of body, comes to the white man's lodge,
> and affirms that he is the white brother whom he saw in his
> dream, and adopts him henceforth. He buries the hatchet
> as it regards his friend, and they hunt and fish and make
> maple-sugar together.[9]

For a time Indian savage and white trader live in harmony
and affection despite the bloodshed between the two races
raging about them. They feel theirs is a chosen, blessed
friendship, for the Indian's dream of their relationship
comes after fasting and solitude. Wawatam has rescued his
white friend from great danger, and he provides a lodge in
which they spend the winter together in great happiness.

> At length, after a long winter of undisturbed and happy
> intercourse...it becomes necessary for Wawatam to take
> leave of his Friend.... "We now exchanged farewells,"

says Henry, "with an emotion entirely reciprocal. I did not quit the lodge without the most grateful sense of the many acts of goodness which I had experienced in it."[10]

Like any dream romance the hiatus cannot last, for it is idyllic, defying time and history. Yet it may cast its spell on the white reader as it did on Thoreau, representing the dream of peace, the romance of how things should have been.

*   *   *   *   *

In order to understand the traditions that inform and give potency to these alternative modes of primitivism, the savage and the natural, one must turn to their roots in gothicism and cultural primitivism. The Gothic Revival of the latter half of the eighteenth century was inspired primarily by the medieval ruin.[11] Moss-grown abbeys, crumbling ruins, and mouldering walls had been so popularized by the "graveyard" poets that their settings and their atmosphere of "somber gloom" became fashionable. The machinery of Gothic literature includes both this deteriorating architecture and a particular attitude toward it. According to Bertrand Evans, Horace Walpole's *The Castle of Otranto* (1764) initiated the genre and gave it two of its central and related ideas, "first, that medieval life was dark, gloomy, and barbarous; second, it would be terrifying if enlightened gentlemen and 'sensible' ladies were transported from contemporary society and suddenly thrust into that earlier time." The Gothic tale's primary intention is to strike terror. The villain's usual function is to frighten young ladies — or, as Evans puts it, "to pursue them through the vaults and labyrinths of the castle, to harass them at every turn," — thus filling the need in the English imagination for an "active agent for terror." He is often tormented by temptation and suffering, by "the beauty and the terror of his bondage to evil."[12]

One effect of the Gothic romances is the substitution of terror for love. The gothicist is bitterly critical of the past; he evokes the olden days not to sentimentalize, but to condemn. This is where he is most in contrast to the cultural primitivist. According to Leslie Fiedler, the Gothic novel wants to prove

> not that its terror is less true than it seems but more true. There *is* a place in men's lives where pictures do in fact bleed, ghosts gibber and shriek, maidens run forever, through serious landscapes from nameless foes; that place is, of course, the world of dreams and of the repressed guilts and fears that motivate them. This world the dogmatic optimism and shallow psychology of the Age of Reason had denied.[13]

As the number of Gothic practitioners grew, so the equipment of the Gothic romance became more extensive. Gothic episodes were soon taking place in caverns, in dark forests, during violent storms, in wild natural settings. Bandits and ghosts became frequent participants. In short, the Gothic romance was at home with any combination of settings, characters, and effects that produced terror in the mind of the reader. "The half-playful, half-pathological evocation of half-believed-in monsters remained for almost a hundred years the West's chief method of dealing with the night-time impulses of the psyche," writes Fiedler.[14]

But how did the Gothic mode of expression, with its basis in Old World ruins and attitudes, get translated into American writing? Our landscapes had no crumbling castles, no ruined abbeys, and our society contained nothing approaching the power of the aristocracy and clergy of England over its middle class.

The emotional appeal of Gothicism is both a compulsion toward and a flight from the terror it evokes. Although America did not have castles, it did have wilderness and savages. The "maiden in flight" convention was easily adaptable to an American setting: she could be chased through the "hideous wilderness" of this despised land. And need one ask by whom? By the villainous savages of the New World, of course, — the Indian or the black man.

Fiedler comments on the ease with which this transition was made, observing that of all the fiction of Western civilization, "our own is most deeply influenced by the Gothic, is almost essentially a Gothic one."[15] Elements of Gothicism pervade American fiction from Charles Brockden Brown to the present day: alienation, flight, spiritual isolation, abysmal fear. Gothicism probably took hold so readily in the American imagination because it replaced the ruling class with the savage figure as chief adversary to settlers in the New World.

Charles Brockden Brown, though by no means a popular success, translated the Gothic novel into American form and exerted considerable influence on its shape and future in American writing. Brown comments in the preface to his novel *Edgar Huntly* (1799) that Gothic castles and chimeras were the objects traditionally employed. But "the incidents of Indian hostility, and the perils of the western wilderness are far more suitable; and, for a native of America to overlook these, would admit of no apology." The Indian is quickly adapted to fill the place of the inquisitor or lecherous nobleman. Brown's Edgar Huntly comments, "I never looked upon or called up the image of a savage, without shuddering."[16] With Brockden Brown, the savage, whether red or black, becomes the chief manifestation of villainy; corruption and evil do not exist in human institutions nearly so much as in nature and its savages. Brown and other American Gothicists have, according to Fiedler, created landscapes that are valid not as they might correspond to externalized landscapes, "but as they correspond in quality to our deepest fears and guilts as projected in our dreams or lived through in 'extreme situations.' "[17]

In *The Savages of America* Roy Harvey Pearce discusses the shift of colonial thinking about the Indian after the 1770s, once it was realized that efforts to Christianize and "civilize" had failed. From this time to the mid-nineteenth century, the image and idea of the Indian as savage dominated the white American mind. To settlers he stood in the path of civilization. To the religious mind he seemed to have fallen irredeemably from his proper human state; surely God "had meant the savage state itself as a sign of Satan's power and savage warfare as a sign of earthly struggle and sin," as Pearce puts it.[18] Opposition of the Indian to the Puritan was seen, allegorically, as Satan's opposition to God. Puritans, with rare exception, were much more interested in what the Indian represented metaphysically (as a warning and negative example to civilization) than culturally.

Although "savagism" ceased to exist as a threat to white civilization after the middle of the nineteenth century, it has continued to captivate the white imagination. It seems likely, however, that for part of the American imagination the black man supplanted the Indian in tales of the Gothic cast. He had, after all, just gained his "freedom" as the red man was being subdued. From their European backgrounds, whites had firmly established the association of blackness with baseness, evil, and death. In order to rationalize slavery's basic denial of human rights, white culture also managed to conceive of blacks as creatures less than human. Cotton Mather, among those staunch Puritan advocates of the Golden Rule, pleaded that "thy Negro is thy Neighbour," but also considered blacks to be brutish and inherently stupid.[19] John Saffin, in his poem "The Negro's Character" (1701), expresses as clearly and directly as any writer the savage mode of the colonial mind:

> Cowardly and cruel, are those *Blacks* Innate,
> Prone to Revenge, Imp of Inveterate hate,
> He that exasperates them; soon espies
> Mischief and Murder in their eyes.
> Libidinous, Deceitful, False and Rude,
> The spume issue of ingratitude.[20]

As Milton Cantor expresses it, for the white colonials it was generally "necessary to find him [the black slave] less a man; to find him a beast, a thing without a soul to lose."[21]

Here, then, are the roots of the savage mode. Suffice it to say that these root attitudes grew and flourished in an increasingly racist soil. Even among the classic writers of the nineteenth century — in Poe's *Pym* and Melville's *Benito Cereno*, for instance — the savage mode is far from absent.[22] Nor did the war that abolished slavery really alter this mode of thought, except perhaps to accelerate it. Indeed, in the latter part of the century, the savage mode proved very popular, as evidenced by the publishing success of Joel Chandler Harris, Thomas Nelson Page, and Thomas Dixon.

Harris presents in his story "Free Joe and the Rest of the World" (1887) a portrait so in contrast to the docility and contentment of his Uncle Remus figure that it deserves attention. Set in 1850, the story contrasts Free Joe, a man who has seemingly turned savage and dangerous in his freedom, with the dancing, singing blacks of slavery.

> Free Joe represented not only a problem of large concern, but, in the watchful eyes of Hillsborough, he was the embodiment of that vague and mysterious danger that seemed to be forever lurking on the outskirts of slavery, ready to sound a shrill and ghostly signal in the impenetrable swamps, and steal forth under the midnight stars to murder, rapine, and pillage, — a danger always threatening, and yet never assuming shape; intangible, and yet real; impossible and yet not improbable. Across the serene and smiling front of safety, the pale outlines of the awful shadow of insurrection sometimes fell.[23]

Harris reflects the ghost of insurrection by making Joe as humble and docile as Uncle Tom, yet loyal and heartbroken in his freedom. For the whites of Hillsborough his harmless freedom became a threatening nightmare, exemplifying the ease and frequency with which the white mind casts black

character in the savage mode. In *Red Rock* (1898), Thomas
Nelson Page does much the same thing, contrasting the
general happiness and peacefulness of black people under
slavery with their transformation, once freed, into brutes
who terrorize the land and rape white women. His volume of
social criticism, *The Negro: The Southerner's Problem* (1904),
justifies lynching as the white South's only means of ending
"the ravishing of their women by an inferior race" which has
turned toward savagery and lust in its new freedom. To
Page, as to Harris and many other white southern writers,
slavery had been a great civilizing agency by constraining
"the Negro's passion, always his controlling force." In its
most obvious form the savage mode includes such blatantly
racist tracts as Thomas Dixon's *The Leopard's Spots* (1902) and
The Clansman (1905). The intention of such writing is to
convince the reader that black people are basically savage,
animalistic creatures who thus deserve a less than human
existence.

*   *   *   *   *

Sigmund Freud and Arthur Lovejoy can help clarify the
meaning of the natural mode of primitivism. In his *Civilization
and Its Discontents* Freud points to the "attitude of primitivism"
that he sees as especially prevalent in the twentieth century,
but also traceable throughout the history of civilized man.
According to such thinking "our so-called civilization itself
is to blame for a great part of our misery, and we should be
much happier if we were to give it up and go back to
primitive conditions."[24] Freud speculates that this attitude of
hostility to civilization resulted principally from the voyages
of discovery, during which civilized man came into contact
with a variety of primitive races and people. He remarks
that "to the Europeans, who failed to observe carefully and
misunderstood what they saw, these people seemed to lead
simple, happy lives — wanting for nothing — such as the

travelers who visited them, with all their superior culture, were unable to achieve."[25] Although the apparent ease of life observed was due in some instances to the bounty of nature, Freud contends that the actual conditions of life were always more difficult than the cultural primitivist imagined.

At the heart of the desire for primitivism is a sentimental impulse toward wish fulfillment stemming from a disregard for many of the facts of existence. Although civilized man would seldom give up his greater measure of security, he looks with longing at the other way of life. Regarding contemporary primitives, Freud reports that, "their instinctual life is by no means to be envied on account of its freedom; it is subject to restrictions of a different kind but perhaps even more rigorous than that of modern civilized man."[26]

Arthur Lovejoy observes that "man has, throughout a great part of his historic march, walked with face turned backward; and a nostalgia for his original state, which tradition and piety had pleasantly idealized, had persistently beset him." Lovejoy distinguishes between chronological and cultural primitivism. The first is

the belief that the earliest condition of man and of human society, *l'homme tel qu'il a du sortir des mains de la Nature*, was the best condition, and this belief, though it encountered opposition from the outset and in nearly all subsequent periods, remained on the whole, for more than twenty-two centuries probably the most widely prevalent preconception about past terrestrial history among Western peoples.[27]

In ancient times and even to the seventeenth century, chronological primitivism was associated with belief in an inevitable decline both in man and nature. It was a common assumption of this line of thought that the worst had yet to come.

It is not a difficult leap from this essentially pessimistic view of civilization to a belief that man could indeed regain

the felicitous state he had once known by returning to his
original way of life and to the earliest forms of society and
government. If such an ideal state once existed, all the more
reason it could exist again. Then the fallen race would
return to nature's ways, which were the ways most "natural"
to man. Lovejoy points out that chronological primitivism,
as a consequence of its great variety of forms, has embraced
the most cheerful meliorism, the gloomiest pessimism, and
various gradations of thought in between.

Cultural primitivism differs from chronological primitivism
in that it elevates as sacred the rustic, the simple, the natural,
but it does not see the need to revert to man's early state for
adequate models. Common to all its strange varieties and
roots is

> the conviction that the time — whatever time may for a
> given writer be in question — is out of joint; that what is
> wrong with it is due to the abnormal complexity and
> sophistication in the life of civilized man, to the patho-
> logical multiplicity and emulativeness of his desires and
> the oppressive over-abundance of his belongings, and the
> factitiousness and want of inner spontaneity of his emotions;
> that "art," the work of man, has corrupted "nature," that is,
> man's own nature; and that the model of the normal
> individual life and the normal social order or at least a
> nearer approximation to it, is to be found among
> contemporary "savage" peoples, whether or not it be
> supposed to have been realized also in the life of primeval
> man.[28]

Lovejoy and Lois Whitney point to the eighteenth century
as seminal for modern attitudes toward cultural primitivism
— the century in which it reached a "climax and a crisis."
Lovejoy comments that

> never before, in modern times, had the praise of the
> simple life sounded quite so eloquently, and with so
> moving an air of conviction, as by Rousseau; and never

before had quite such seemingly engaging models of the noble savage and the life according to nature been available for primitivistic uses as after the French and British voyages of exploration among the Polynesian peoples in the 1700's and 1770's.[29]

The great increase in publishers and readers spread the idea, while primitivists such as Diderot, Rousseau, and Morelly vigorously attacked the economic and political systems of the period. And the new fashion of "sensibility" in the latter half of the century had in its preference for natural instincts and actions a close affinity to primitivism.

But the eighteenth century was also a period when new events and tendencies of thought were working against primitivism more vigorously than ever before. Throughout the century, the concepts of "progress" and the "growth of civilization" were finding increasingly frequent expression as axioms of the historic process. Although primitivism slowly gave ground to these overpowering forces, it gained a certain heightened appeal in doing so. The child of nature and the rustic type seemed, by consequence, the more precious.

American primitivism, when in the natural mode, has been more often cultural than chronological. This mode of thought, in its sentimental regard for the land and the natural man, blatantly disregards the brutal circumstances under which red and black people have been forced to live in America. Writers in this mode characteristically fail to distinguish between their sentimentality for a particular way of life and the facts of white America's sacrifice or subjugation of Indians, its slavery and exploitation of blacks.

A rather harmless example of the idealization of Indians and blacks as "natural men" comes from Robert Beverley's *History and Present State of Virginia* (1705). This astute planter and historian describes Indians as unspoiled creatures, as pure as the virgin land they inhabit, neither

debauch'd nor corrupted with the Pomps and Vanities,
which had depraved and inslaved the Rest of Mankind.[30]

Beverley describes an American Eden in which the Indians
are the unfallen sons of Adam. He pictures them as
generally admirable people — happy, faithful, generous —
and he observes that his civilization is "hardly making
Improvements equivalent to that Damage" it brings to the
Indians and the New World Garden.[31]

The adjectives Beverley uses to portray Indians in
eighteenth-century Virginia are strikingly similar to those
used to describe slaves in the novels of the antebellum
South, despite the differences in time and subject. John
Pendleton Kennedy and other writers of the plantation
tradition describe this way of life in terms of the pastoral
ideal, with the "garden" its root metaphor. Unlike Beverley,
these writers do not admit that in creating its pastoral ideal
white civilization violated both the land and the people they
enslaved to work it. As long as blacks remained passive,
cooperative, and loyal, they were assumed to be "happy," to
be benefiting from the "advantages" of white civilization.
John Pendleton Kennedy's *Swallow Barn* (1832), usually
regarded as the most "vivid" picture of the Old Dominion
before the war, sets something of a model for those works of
the plantation tradition that follow it. Presenting a thoroughly
romantic picture of slavery — human kindness in the owners
and contentment among the blacks — Kennedy sees slaves as
childlike and "picturesque." In reviewing *Swallow Barn* Poe
amplifies this attitude, commenting that

> we shall take leave to speak...of loyal devotion on the
> part of the slave to which the white man's heart is a
> stranger, and of the master's reciprocal feeling of parental
> attachment to his humble dependent.... That these
> sentiments in the breast of the Negro and the master are
> stronger than they would be under like circumstances
> between individuals of the white race, we believe.[32]

In "The Gold Bug" (1834) Poe takes for granted the "happy relationship" between the slave Jupiter and his master. William Gilmore Sims goes a step further in *The Yemassee* (1835), describing the slave Hector who so loved his master that he refused freedom when it was offered him.[33]

Postbellum sentimentalizations of the same slave-master relationship can be found throughout Thomas Nelson Page, Irwin Russell, and Joel Chandler Harris.[34] Whether before the war or after, these portraits hardly ever refer to blacks working in the fields. Usually they are singing and dancing, hunting possum, telling stories in the quarter, or tending their gardens. They seem to have abundant leisure. Their holidays are often described at considerable length, and always the assumed background is of the plantation as a garden, an American version of Eden.[35]

As for the white southern writers of the next generation (Julia Peterkin, Paul Green, Ellen Glasgow, and DuBose Heyward), V. F. Calverton quite accurately sees them as writing out of the natural mode of primitivism.

> The Negro alone, living in a different world of motivation, has retained enough of his simplicity and charm and irresponsible gaiety to attract writers for the next genera-tion.... While the white man's world, spiked in on every side by religious ramparts, has become desolate of religious cultural stimulus, the black man's world has taken on fresh meaning.... Only the old Negro whose life is still uncorrupted...arouses the interest and sympathy of this new school of authors. In this sense, however successfully they have managed to avoid the sentimentalities of the old plantation school, these writers are much closer to the plantation than they suspect.[36]

Even though Calverton's choice of words ("uncorrupted," "simplicity and charm," "irresponsible gaiety") suggests a personal, perhaps unconscious attachment to the stereotypes of the Old South, his comments help one see the connection of white southern writers of this century with certain attitudes toward blacks rooted in the plantation tradition.

In general, portraits in the natural mode are of spontaneous, uninhibited people, untainted by white civilization and embued with a certain "rustic wisdom." They entertain, educate, and lend assistance to civilized visitors, and possess a certain almost innate goodness of spirit and deed. One is continually surprised at the absence of change or conflict, at the general stasis and lack of tension in the lives of figures handled in the natural mode. Blacks or whites, they seem content with their lives; they are unaware of either social upheaval or racial conflict. If the forces that produce tension or change are at work in the literature of the natural mode, the natural figures themselves are unaware of them.

While the savage figure is usually a malevolent activist and a threat to society, his or her natural counterpart is ill-suited for dramatic action and is more often found in fable, legend, myth, and idyl. Black naturals are seen in half-light, in bas-relief; their elusive, symbolic forms do not bear up under careful scrutiny. Blacks as savage figures are politically and ideologically ambitious; they build empires, promulgate religions, lust for wealth and sex. Their very activity is a threat to white civilization, which in part explains the need of the "civilized" to subdue them.

While the savage is crafty and seductive, natural figures are never people of duplicity; they live quietly and reverently in the bosom of nature. Civilized society can find special pleasure in fraternizing with them, knowing they are harmless and unambitious. White society's traditional attitudes toward the savage vis-à-vis the natural are quickly apparent: the savages are threatening, but the naturals are a pleasure. The old clichés — "The only good Indian is a dead Indian" and "There are only two types of Niggers: good and bad" — are painfully pertinent here. As Pearce has pointed out, the white man made the Indian fit his image of the savage in order to justify massacre. Similarly, blacks who cooperated with whites, whether before or after slavery, were "good

Niggers" and "noble fellows"; those who did not were crazed or savages, the blood of the jungle still in their veins.

2.   The Savages

His thick lips were drawn upward in an ugly leer and
his sinister bead eyes gleamed like a gorilla's. A single
fierce leap and the black claws clutched the air slowly as
if sinking into the soft white throat.
                          Thomas Dixon, *The Clansman*

Mumbo-Jumbo is dead in the jungle.
Never again will he hoo-doo you.
Never again will he hoo-doo you.
                          Vachel Lindsay, "The Congo"

After the Civil War the numerous antebellum descriptions
of docile, contented slaves gave way to the stereotype termed
by Sterling Brown as "the Brute Negro."[1] Brown refers to
works ranging from the post-war period well into the
twentieth century that are devoted to promulgating a
concept of black savagism and inferiority. Among these are
Josiah Priest's *The Bible Defense of Slavery* (1851), H. R.
Helper's *Nojoque* (1867), and Charles Carroll's *The Negro a
Beast* (1900). All three emphasize the alleged beastly qualities
of black people. As previously mentioned, Thomas Dixon's
The Leopard's Spots and *The Clansman* are among the most
blatant examples of the savage mode used for racist effect. In
both novels there are scenes inspired by the Gothic in which
a black man, huge and gorilla-like, attacks and rapes a "fair
white damsel." In each case the Clan rides in revenge,
upholding the "honor of white southern womanhood."
DuBose Heyward is hardly comparable to Thomas Dixon,

but his *The Half Pint Flask* (1929) is a chilling tale of the pursuit and murder of a white man by black "natives" on a remote Carolina island.

Not all literature of the savage mode is this direct or obvious in its intention. Dixon's technique was too blatant, too obviously propagandistic to attract many writers. Yet a number of white writers have been attracted by the subtler possibilities of the savage mode and have found its themes popular among their readers. Even if the Gothic framework and jungle-like settings are abandoned, the message may remain much the same: blacks are innately savage people. It is a state of mind that takes pleasure in seeing blacks in the jungle rather than in rural and urban settings, that thrills at the description of a medicine man, an animal god, dancing natives, or a tom-tom beat. This mental stance is, in short, a quasi-savagism, or, to use Pearce's phrase, a "gentle, civilized terror in the presence of the savage,"[2] and may in fact appeal emotionally to many who would reject it rationally.

Stephen Crane, Vachel Lindsay, and Eugene O'Neill were attracted by the savage mode. Lindsay's "The Congo" expresses many of the fascinations with exotic Africana just mentioned, as well as a strong Christian chauvinism. O'Neill's *The Emperor Jones* also exploits the jungle motif, describing the atavistic regression of a "civilized" black man to his previously "savage state." As will be observed, the savage mode facilitates a disguised presentation of many racially pejorative statements and stereotypes. Some writers, notably Crane and Waldo Frank, present a bifurcated consciousness: the savagism of a white society and, in ironic contrast, the more enlightened perspective of a narrative voice, or the first-hand experience of a black character.

STEPHEN CRANE

Stephen Crane's "The Monster" (1897) provides the occasion

for scrutiny of an early and major work of the modern period that elaborates the savage mode. Crane's portrait of the black coachman Henry Johnson is a far cry from the blatantly racist portraits of writers such as Thomas Dixon and Charles Carroll. Crane brings to this work the complexity of theme, finely honed irony, and depths of human compassion associated with the best of his writing. In "The Monster" he attempts to distinguish between the savagery of civilized whites in their reaction to a disfigured black man and the very unsavage, unmonsterlike reality of his life.

At the time of its publication William Dean Howells gave the novella high praise, although many other critics have disfavored it.[3] In a perceptive contemporary discussion of the novella, Donald Gibson has termed it "in certain respects...the most ambitious piece Crane ever attempted."[4] It is, as Gibson and many others have commented, Crane's most critical portrait of society. Not only does the story reveal the pettiness, the ingrained fears, and prejudices of white America, it provides a dilemma through which to test the moral fiber of a man of principle. This man is Dr. Trescott, physician in the town of Whilomville, New York, and Stephen Crane's portrait of a "good man," a man even Christlike in character.[5] The second hero of the novel is Henry Johnson, Dr. Trescott's black coachman, who saves the good doctor's son by carrying him through the burning inferno of the Trescott house. Charles Mayer expresses the heroic twinship of employer and employee in this way: Trescott's "moral act is the counterpoint of Henry's physical heroism."[6] The thrust of most discussions of "The Monster," however, has been to examine the interplay between Trescott and the Whilomville community and largely to overlook the hero and "villain" of the story, Henry Johnson.

Crane holds a key position in *Savages and Naturals* because of his "primary interest in the plight of the individual."[7] The issue here is how sensitively does this brilliant social realist portray the black servant who is the focal center of his novel? Is Crane able to establish and maintain a counter-distinction between public opinion of his character and the complex, anguished, private reality of this man? It is not enough to say that Crane attempted a difficult task in exploring race relations and moral values; the final test will be of Crane's own integrity to the character of Henry Johnson. One may turn to Ralph Ellison's *Invisible Man* or Richard Wright's *Native Son* for comparison. Ellison and Wright, it should be said, never lose sight of their protagonists while describing the reactions of white society to them.

In the opening pages of "The Monster" Crane attempts to provide a detailed and individual portrait of Henry Johnson. Henry and Dr. Trescott's son Jimmy are best of friends. Crane comments, "He grinned fraternally when he saw Jimmie coming. These two were pals. In regard to almost everything in life they seemed to have minds precisely alike."[8] The insertion of "seems" saves the description from racist assumptions. The reader soon learns that Henry is more than a "pal"; he is able to console Jimmy when the boy is in trouble with his father, and even to mediate between the two. In the evenings, when Henry dresses up for town, Crane writes that he "was more like a priest arraying himself for some parade of the church." He puts on lavender trousers and dons a straw hat with a bright silk band. To his author, Henry is not a comic or ludicrous figure. Forced by society to an inferior position, he can at best imitate white society and pretend he is a gentleman. "There was no cake-walk hyperbole in it. He was simply a quiet, well-bred gentleman of position, wealth, and other achievements out for an evening's stroll" (434). Like "Nigger Jim" and Huck Finn, Henry and Jimmy are pals, but Henry is also seen here as an adult and an actor who shifts roles frequently to make the best of his situation as a black man in a town like Whilomville.

The power of Crane's irony becomes apparent now. Henry's reception by the townsfolk stands in contrast to the portrait of him Crane has just drawn. One white man hails him with, "Hello, Henry! Going to walk for a cake tonight?" Further down the block another comments, "Why, you've got the cake right in your pocket, Henry!" (435) Crane's intention in these comments is not certain until later in the story when his satire of the white townsfolk becomes unmistakable. The whites here are obviously not responding to the Henry Johnson whom Crane has just described but to their ingrained minstrel image of a black man "dressed up" for their entertainment rather than his own. Henry seems accustomed to this treatment; it is the way of Whilomville.

Even though Henry is among the first to reach the burning Trescott house, flames are already "roaring like a winter wind among the pines." He rushes up the flaming staircase, but by the time he has gotten little Jim, the staircase is engulfed in flames. After a moment of hesitation and panic, he recalls the back stairway that leads down and out through Dr. Trescott's laboratory. Once down the stairs, he pushes open the door to confront a garden of burning flowers:

Flames of violet, crimson, green, blue, orange, and purple were blooming everywhere. . . .
Johnson halted for a moment on the threshold. He cried out again in the negro wail that had in it the sadness of the swamps. Then he rushed across the room. . . . There was an explosion at one side, and suddenly before him there reared a delicate, trembling sapphire shape like a fairy lady. With a quiet smile she blocked his path and doomed him and Jimmie. Johnson shrieked, and then ducked in the manner of his race in fights. He aimed to pass under the left guard of the sapphire lady. But she was swifter than eagles, and her talons caught in him as he plunged past her. Bowing his head as if his neck had been struck, Johnson lurched forward, twisting this way and that way. He fell on his back. The still form in the blanket flung from his arms, rolled to the edge of the floor and beneath the window. (441-442)

Crane's portrait of Henry Johnson was based on his recollection of a black man named Levi Hume " 'who hauled ashes in Port Jervis. His face had been eaten by cancer. He was an object of horror to the children there,' says one of Crane's nieces, 'for it could truthfully be said of him, 'he had no face.' " [9] One may presume, then, that the burning laboratory was Crane's invention. The great horror of the scene comes from the realization that it represents a domestic jungle that Henry, like O'Neill's Emperor Jones, must cross in order to survive. The panther flame that leaps at him, the sapphire flame of the "fairy lady," the ruby-eyed, "scintillant and writhing serpent" (442) may be seen as various manifestations of racism and inhumanity harbored in the "good" people of Whilomville. The jeers and taunts hurled at "supremely good-natured" Henry earlier in the evening were prelude to this scene and are contained in it. The flaming jungle is neither Hell nor Africa, but a white physician's laboratory. The implied savagism refers not to the black man, Henry, but to the townsfolk in their reactions to Henry's disfigurement. Crane's intended effect here is quite the opposite of the jungle portraits presented by Vachel Lindsay and Eugene O'Neill. The "writing serpent" represents the sin of racial injustice, or more generally, all acts that debase character and subvert honest relations.

At Trescott's insistence, Henry is brought forth, "a thing which he laid on the grass." From this point on, even Crane begins referring to Henry with increasing detachment. It is at first puzzling and disturbing that Henry is maimed in the laboratory of the man whom Crane admires most among the people of Whilomville. Crane chooses to test Trescott precisely because he sees admirable qualities in the man. Trescott is the only character in "The Monster" who might have wisdom, humanity, and strength of character sufficient to maintain integrity and understanding during the events that follow.

The "Morning Tribune," which had sent a boy up hourly

to see if Henry had yet died, finally goes to press announcing his death. Now that it seems likely he will not live, people begin referring to him as "a saint." Crane implies through this sentiment not only that a society desires to kill its heroes so that it may properly praise them, but that to the white community there is something especially noble in the sacrificial death of a black man while saving a white child. It would be comforting for the whites to believe both that blacks were born to serve and that Henry and "his race" also recognized white superiority and were willing to sacrifice their lives to protect it.[10]

In contrast to the town's hero worship, Crane gives a very different scene at Judge Hagenthorpe's house, where Henry had been taken after the fire. His head and body, frightfully burned, are covered in bandages; all that is visible is "an eye, which unwinkingly stared at the judge." Trescott sleeps and eats at the judge's house, keeping an almost continuous vigil, doing what he can to facilitate Henry's recovery. In his desire to do the medically "right" thing, to save a life, Trescott does not consider the possible mental and physical disfigurement that might attend Henry's survival.

The judge has considered these possibilities, and comments to Trescott: " 'He will hereafter be a monster, a perfect monster' " (448). Later he adds, as his mind begins to work on the subject, " 'He will be your creation, you understand. He is purely your creation. Nature has evidently given him up. He is dead. You are restoring him to life. You are making him, and he will be a monster and with no mind' " (448). Perhaps, as the judge argues, Trescott errs in struggling to save Henry. It is clear from his reply he is working partially out of self-interest. " 'He will be what you like, Judge,' cried Trescott, in a sudden polite fury, 'He will be anything, but, by God! he saved my boy' " (449). Not once does he consider the kind of life Henry could have or where he will live and who will care for him. Could the judge's comment that Trescott's act is one of the "blunders of virtue" be Crane's criticism of the doctor, despite his admiration for the man? As Hagenthorpe said, the Henry Johnson once known is dead and what emerges from the ashes depends on one's perspective. To the judge he is a blunder of indiscriminate healing; to the doctor he is a savior; to the town he is a monster.

Crane's metaphor of facelessness is analogous to Ralph Ellison's metaphor of invisibility. The former Henry Johnson is no longer, and in his stead society places its desired substitutes. "He now had no face. His face had simply been burned away," and in its place whites and blacks substitute the masks they desire. Yet his physical facelessness also brings into focus that virtual facelessness he quiety tolerated in the white community before the fire. In the passing scenes, as this process occurs, Crane juxtaposes the innocence of Henry with the monstrous inhumanity of Whilomville.

Not only is the doctor's practice dwindling as a result of gossip about Henry, but insults and threats are hurled at the family. One of his neighbors moves away in protest. Next, Trescott is visited by a self-appointed committee of four of the town's "very active and influential citizens." They have come, they say, out of friendship and concern, lest he "ruin himself" over this "silly" matter. Their message is, in essence: even if there are a lot of fools in Whilomville stirring up this mess, it is senseless for you to "ruin yourself by opposing them. You can't teach them anything, you know" (473). The members of the committee pose a considerable threat to Trescott's position, for they appear as the voices of reason and good sense. Instead, they are the voices of rationalization. Before their scrutiny all issues of moral judgment dissolve into matters of practicality and profitability. John Twelve, a prosperous grocer, offers Trescott "a little no-good farm up beyond Clarence Mountain" on which Henry could live out his days in seclusion. Trescott refuses the offer and the committee departs. Is Crane not suggesting in the "little no-good farm" the patronizing charity "well-intentioned" whites have so often offered "cooperative" blacks?

In Crane's world survival is difficult; survival with integrity is almost impossible. The condition of warfare is all-pervasive in his fiction. In fact, it is Crane's richest symbol for man's condition. As in *The Red Badge of Courage* and "The Open Boat," Crane is interested here in studying man under stress. In all three works, as Sy Kahn has observed, "forging and tempering an answerable courage and code is the repetitive situation."[11] If Trescott is as strong as he seems, he and his family will manage with Henry under their care, despite the town.

What is most regrettable about "The Monster," however, is Crane's shift in emphasis in the latter half, from Henry to Dr. Trescott. For all his care to avoid stereotyping Henry, Crane retreats further and further from him as the story progresses. By the end he is almost a forgotten character, totally absent from the last ten pages of the novella. From the time of the fire, neither Crane nor his readers get near Henry again. First an unblinking eye stares out from beneath bandages, then the reader hears reports of what he has done, what he looks like, as observed from windows, open doors, porches, from the corner of a barn. As a result, Henry is removed from the center of our vision, and almost from our concern. The finely honed irony of contrast between the Henry whom Crane described and the Henry seen by the white townsfolk is lost in the latter half of "The Monster." The reader does not know if his face is really as hideous as described, or what humanity remains beneath the "faceless" face. For the reader Henry Johnson has become an invisible man.

Why does Crane retreat from his focus on Henry and shift his attention to Trescott? Had he created a creature he could no longer work with? Had he created, in fact, a monster rather than the outward visage of a monster? Or is Crane, the supreme ironist, not only in control of his craft but intentionally testing the reader's identification and sympathy? Perhaps he intended "The Monster" to read us, to see whether his readers sided emotionally with Whilomville, even if intellectually with Dr. Trescott.

The Stallman biography of Crane documents the notion that " 'The Monster' was an appeal for brotherhood between white and black."[12] In a very limited sense the story achieves this end — the fidelity of Trescott to Henry *is* admirable — but at great expense in its development and handling of black character. Unfortunately, most commentary on "The Monster" has forgotten to look at Crane's other black portraits or to consider the novella's treatment of race. Stallman, at least, observed that "Crane's social irony is that the white man's face is also disfigured — by white society's cruelty to the Negro."[13] Ralph Ellison has commented that "there is no question as to the Negro's part in it, nor to the fact that the issues go much deeper than the question of race."[14] Only the latter half of Ellison's statement would seem to be true: there are several serious questions to be raised concerning black character in the story.

During Crane's now somewhat famous luncheon at Ravensbrook, Harold Frederick attacked and Crane passionately defended "The Monster"; Sanford Bennett, Crane's other guest, politely defended him. Later Bennett commented that he was "for years troubled by a memory of the Negro's shattered visage."[15] What bothered him is the line "He had no face." This is precisely the novella's problem. The literal fire and disfigurement are to stand for the real, though often disguised, injuries suffered particularly by black Americans. Yet after the fire Crane does not restore Henry for the reader. He does not distinguish between the symbolic disfigurement of Henry represented by the actual injuries and the Henry who must reside beneath the "monster" if one is to continue identifying with him. This is where Crane fails. There is nothing left of Henry for the reader to identify with; he is figuratively dead. Consequently one must shift identification and sympathy to Dr. Trescott.

Briefly consider Henry during his visit to the black community after his injury. Crane describes him here and through the remainder of the tale as "the monster," "it," "the terror"; he has Henry raise a "deprecatory claw" while addressing the Farragut women. Although they see him as the monster they have been warned about, Crane presents Henry's speech in minstrel fashion. Henry Johnson makes a succession of low and sweeping bows, scraping his feet and mumbling,

> "Don't make no botheration 'bout me, Miss Fa'gut... No 'deed. I jes' drap in ter ax you if I can have the magnifercent gratitude of you' company on that 'casion, Miss Fa'gut." (460)

Instead of suffering from shock, one sees that Henry has been reduced by Crane to the comic Sambo stereotype. Yet to the other blacks of "Watermelon Alley" he has been transformed into a monster. In their desperation to get away from Henry the black residents shriek and screech; one of them even breaks her leg attempting to scale a fence. Regrettably, Crane chose to use familiar stereotypes rather than attempt the much more difficult task of detailing Henry's mental and physical injury while maintaining his humanity and individuality.

Crane's description of Alek Williams, the black man who tended Henry for a time, is even more derisive. Alek is obviously Crane's attempt at a comic black portrait. He is described as obsessively superstitious, inexcusably lazy, and continually amusing. He asks for more money from Judge Hagenthorpe because his frightened children cannot eat. They imagine Henry to be the devil. Alek stands before the judge, "scratching his wool, and beating his knee with his hat." While arguing for a raise, he "began swinging his head from side to side in the strange racial mannerism" (153). The portrait, with its comic touches and its racial generalizations, is unnecessary for the story's development and is inexcusable.

The only other glimpse of the much-altered Henry Johnson occurs in chapter twenty, where Jimmie Trescott leads his companions to the edge of the Trescott barn so they can gape at Johnson. Crane writes that Jim slowly "sidled into closer relations with *it*," referring to Henry, but fails to show even a hint of the old friendship. On a dare, Jim runs up and touches Henry. "*The monster* was crooning a weird line of negro melody that was scarcely more than a thread of sound, and *it* paid no heed to the boy" (my italics, 468). This is the reader's last glimpse of Henry Johnson. It is as if in his mental derangement he were slipping back in time, becoming more thoroughly a primitive figure. He croons softly and submits to his condition. Crane made this same point while describing the fire. "He was submitting, submitting because of his fathers, bending his mind in a most perfect slavery to this conflagration" (441). During the fire Henry chose to act and resisted the flames while he could. But now Crane has rendered him incapable of either understanding his plight or of resisting it. Whatever is to be done for Henry must either be done by the Trescotts of Crane's world or it will be done by the fools of Whilomville.

Crane's blacks are both comics and fools. They are static, ineffectual creatures, dependent upon white beneficence, where it exists, and mindlessly copying white culture. Crane is not to be faulted for speculating that the black community would also fail to respond to Henry with sympathy and brotherhood. That is a plausible assessment of human nature, black or white. What is so blatant is Crane's own racism. It is Crane, after all, who refers to Alek Williams's hair as "wool," to Henry's hand as a "claw," and who stages a minstrel scene on the Farragut porch. These touches are at the expense of black character and have nothing to do with their moral failure to see Henry's great need.

Several critics have considered "The Monster" a problem

story, lacking in unity,[16] but not for the reasons indicated here. Stallman says of Crane, "No white American author has pictured a Negro performing a truly heroic act before Crane did it in "The Monster.""[17] He overlooks Mrs. Stowe's Uncle Tom, Melville's Daggoo, and many other examples. More important, however, it is virtually impossible to see Henry, at the conclusion of "The Monster," as a "truly heroic" figure. He is a pathetic figure, and even one's pity is mitigated by his apparent contentment and inability to comprehend his plight. Rather, the heroic portrait is of Trescott, a good man struggling against awesome odds to preserve his moral integrity. Henry is ultimately to be seen as a foil in Crane's testing of the moral fiber and resolve of his white doctor.

The regrettable, though inescapable conclusion is that Crane's "monster" got away from him. He could no longer work with Henry, except at considerable distance, because he had lost the critical distinction he started with — between the monster mask and the man beneath the mask. By the end of the novella there is only mask; somewhere along the way the man had ceased to be. Even though Crane fails to sustain the portrait of Henry, his novella remains a very significant failure. Crane is most skillful, after all, in exposing the potential savagism of Whilomville toward blacks and all scapegoats, and it appears that he intended a fully developed and sustained portrait of Henry. Yet one must judge what is, not what might have been. Crane's portrait of Henry Johnson reflects an artistic maladroitness in handling a character who demanded utmost care, and in a piece of fiction otherwise finely wrought. Further, it reflects a sadly limited racial consciousness, despite all good intentions, in one of America's most astute and compassionate social realists.

VACHEL LINDSAY

Vachel Lindsay's enormously popular poem, "The Congo" (1914), operates from a racial premise quite the opposite of Crane's in "The Monster." Crane's Henry Johnson was a heroic black man who risked his life to save a white boy from fire. Horribly disfigured by the flames, Henry seems to become a savage in the irrational and racist perspective of Crane's community. By contrast, Lindsay shows the conversion of Africans from "their basic savagery" into a Christian and childlike society. Lindsay's focus is on collective, rather than individual, black portraits. The poem also reveals his racist belief that blacks are a lesser race that could be redeemed by conversion and by their "natural" potential for "music and mirth." Lindsay capitalizes on the great popularity of Africa as a subject matter, incorporating various stereotyped images of Africa from white popular culture. He purports to dramatize the death of the very source of savagery, the Voodoo gods and priests, and to picture an Africa free of their "terrible" influence.

The January 1913 issue of *Poetry* opened with Lindsay's "General William Booth Enters into Heaven." This was a great event for the poet, and contrary to his earlier poems, it was well received. In it he forged that combination of noisy brashness, strong rhythms, and sentiment that is at the center of his most popular poems, including "The Congo." Harriet Monroe, editor of *Poetry*, found its freshness, vitality, and moral fervor a desirable contrast to the poems of Yeats, Pound, and Tagore that she had been publishing.

Lindsay saw the poem as more than a tribute to the deceased Salvation Army General. "It was a universal affirmation of the goodness of man and the humaneness of Christ. 'Whoever tries to make a cynic of me is wasting his breath...*I believe* in the human race.'"[18] As "General Booth" portrays the salvation of the heathen masses from America's urban jungles, "The Congo" depicts salvation of African savages. By the end of the poem, the Congo is converted into a valley of "paradise" by the twelve apostles and their pioneer angels.

Reviewers and public quickly took to the "high vaudeville" style — as Lindsay called it — of "General Booth." After years of frustrated apprenticeship he felt he had at last found a style that would draw attention and sell poems. He admitted it was the trick devices and bold rhythms of "General Booth" that made it such a popular success. Little wonder the poems that followed ("Calliope" and "The Congo") were written, quite deliberately, to capitalize on the success achieved in "General Booth." While "The Congo" was in progress, Lindsay wrote that he was working on "a Congo piece that will make the Calliope look like thirty cents. Every kind of war-drum ever heard. Then the Minstrel's Heaven. Then a glorious Camp Meeting. Boomlay Boomlay Boomlay Boom!" (210). Although Lindsay admitted a personal dislike for vaudeville and even for this element of his poetry, he saw in its gaudiness a way of gettng to the public. As Eleanor Ruggles puts it, "He began to see that poetic superstructures could be raised on this primitive foundation" (211). Lindsay's imagination was much taken with the exotic and the primitive. Of making a poem in this manner, he commented, "One composes it not by listening to the inner voice and following the gleam — but by pounding the table with a ruler and looking out the window at the electric signs" (211).

Lindsay's concepts of Africa and of black people in general can be traced to several events in his childhood. His mother read frequently to him from Grimm's *Fairy Tales*, and his father often read aloud from *Uncle Remus*. Poe's Gothicism — his exotic settings and strange tales — made him seem very "Egyptian" to Lindsay. In addition to the tales of contented slaves and miserable freedmen to be encountered in the *Remus* tales, Lindsay probably became acquainted with Poe's much more corrosive black portraits in "The Gold Bug" and *Pym*.

One of Lindsay's favorite books was Stanley's *In Darkest Africa*. Ruggles describes the particular edition Lindsay owned as having for its cover decoration a map of Africa all in black on which was traced with a heavy gold line the course of the Congo (42). Here was the inspiration for the most celebrated couplet he ever composed:

THEN I SAW THE CONGO, CREEPING THROUGH THE BLACK,
CUTTING THROUGH THE FOREST WITH A GOLDEN TRACK.

It is difficult to be sure of other influences on "The Congo." One source is the song "My Castle on the Nile" that, ironically enough, the black singer Bert Williams had made popular just at the time Lindsay was putting together "The Congo." Williams's lines "Inlaid diamonds on de flo',/ A baboon butler at mah do' " (212) seems too similar to Lindsay's "baboon butler in the agate door" to be unrelated. There are other images of black life from this country and abroad that may have influenced Lindsay. He heard the Hampton singers in an evening of spirituals and witnessed the dancers of Dahomey perform at the Chicago World's Fair. Raymond Purkey, in his biorgraphy of Lindsay, states that the poet had read Mark Twain's attack on King Leopold, *King Leopold's Soliloquy* (1905) and W.E.B. DuBois's *The Souls of Black Folk* (1903).[19] It is also known that Lindsay had read Conrad's *Heart of Darkness* (1899). The centrality of the river to Conrad's tale ("one river especially, a mighty big river . . . resembling an immense snake uncoiled") seems a likely influence, as does Conrad's association of blackness and darkness with evil.

The most direct and immediate inspiration for the poem came during a service one Sunday in October 1913 at the First Christian Church of Springfield. "The minister, Brother Burnham, spoke sadly from the pulpit of the death by drowning in the River Congo of his old college friend,

Brother Ray Eldred, a missionary" (212). Suddenly two powerful themes in Lindsay's life fused: his long-standing interest in Africa and his love for the Christian church — including its zealous missionary enterprises abroad. The death of a missionary, while trying to bring to Africa what Lindsay and many Christians imagined to be the hope and salvation of the Christian West, was perfect subject matter for a major poem. Ruggles comments:

> Lindsay was sitting with his parents in their pew in the third row when suddenly all the panorama of the Negro race flashed into his mind. He remembered from his childhood the pious ecstasies of black Lucy, their cook. He remembered the [black] waiters around the woodpile at the Leland rocked by laughter as by a force outside themselves. He remembered Charlie Gibbs, Springfield's gigantic Negro lawyer, who was surely born to prance on the riverbank with a coffin-headed shield and a shovel spear. (212)

In attempting to capture the powerful emotions that no doubt came together in Lindsay's mind during that church service, Eleanor Ruggles almost manages to convince herself that what Lindsay imagined at this point in time and what he subsequently presented in "The Congo" was indeed "A Study of the Negro Race," rather than a threadbare collection of exotic images and clichés.

Although legend has it that Lindsay came home from church and dashed off "The Congo" before dinner, its writing and revisions actually took him two months. His first public performance of the poem, at Springfield's Lincoln Day banquet in 1914, was received with amazement turning to laughter. His friends and relatives were mortified. During his presentation they saw "his hands shoot from the cuffs of his dress suit and jab the air; his body rock and his shoulders sway to the tom-tom beat of, 'Mumbo-Jumbo, God of the Congo' " (215). Even though the Springfield audience

disliked the poem, the staff and friends of *Poetry* who
gathered a month later in Chicago to honor Yeats received
"The Congo" warmly. "The audience burst into applause.
The Negro waiters against the walls applauded"[20] (218).

Trying to explain to his Springfield friends who had so
disliked the poem, Lindsay wrote in the *State Register* that he
hoped to portray the concern of a savage, childlike race with
religion. The religion would save its soul. The "Mumbo-
Jumbo" theme represents the "ill fate and sinister power of
Africa from the beginning," which he saw as mitigated by
what he considered a racial proclivity for music, mirth, and
joy. There was also in the black race, he believed, great
capacity for emotion and vision: "Thinking of this gives us
too a vision," Lindsay comments, "a picture of that race
redeemed through the inner impulse developed in its
highest form" (214).

The poem is divided into three parts: "I. Their Basic
Savagery," "II. Their Irrepressible High Spirits," and "III.
The Hope of Their Religion." Part I may be subdivided into
three portions, two of which describe the drunken revelry
and dangerous savagery Lindsay imagines to be at the center
of African life. The middle portion, by contrast, describes
the narrator's vision:

> Then I had religion. Then I had a vision.
> I could not turn from their revel in derision.
> THEN I SAW THE CONGO, CREEPING
> THROUGH THE BLACK,
> CUTTING THROUGH THE FOREST WITH A
> GOLDEN TRACK.

The second couplet of this stanza forms the refrain of the
poem, and is repeated in parts II and III. Just before the
narrator's vision, he has been witnessing a bout of African-
styled, drunken revelry. There is nothing prior to the
refrain that convinces the reader of "Their Basic Savagery."
It is a good, lively tavern scene. There is much pounding on

tables; several drunks stagger and reel about, but there is not even a good tussle. The participants are termed "Fat black bucks," and "Barrel-house kings" who do their savage beating with broom handles and silk umbrellas. The stereotyped image is that of the pretentious black reveler, who loves silks and liquor (good living) and who, when drunk, imagines himself a king. Similar stereotyped portraits of the "pompous Negro" can be found in the novels of Kennedy and Simms and elsewhere in the figure of the Minstrel Dandy. The third portion continues the basic imagery of the first. The "tatooed cannibals" are worked up to "blood-lust" pitch. Witch doctors bring them to a frenzy of a war dance. Now they will hurl their voodoo curses, and "steal the pygmies...kill the Arabs...kill the white man." Portion three ends with a warning, presumably because of the death of Brother Eldred:

> Be careful what you do,
> Or Mumbo-Jumbo, God of the Congo,
> ...will hoo-doo you.

Taken as a whole, Part I reveals that Africans are not just pretentious drunks prancing crazily about but dangerous savages when incited by the evil priests of their religion. The witch-doctors are clearly the villains of the poem. They shake rattles, hurl curses, and induce violence.

The stated subject of Part II is "Their Irrepressible High Spirits," but the scene is a pastiche of references to Africa and America. Now the Congo is a "minstrel river," perhaps the Mississippi, where "crap-shooters" and revelers dance the juba and "cake-walk princes" cavort. They wear long red coats, tall silk hats, and "shoes with a patent leather shine." This "happy" scene suggests the fusion in Lindsay's mind of a white stereotyped version of black experience in Africa and America.

Although Lindsay called his style "high vaudeville," so

many of the clichés of the minstrel tradition appear that it might better be termed "high minstrel." The coal-black maidens have bells on their ankles and feet. A "scalawag" royalty steps out the cake-walk. It is, Lindsay writes, a "Negro fairyland" where "dreams come true." Dominating the scene is an ebony palace with porches inlaid in ivory, gold, and elephant bone. A "parrot band" provides the music for Lindsay's Afro-American minstrel fantasy. The throng of revelers in the palace court "dance the juba from wall to wall." Although there are no "blood-lust" songs, the witch-men still make their appearance. They are "skull-faced" and wear long-tailed coats, and hats covered with "diamond-dust." At one point the witch-men still the throng with stern glares and their old song, "Mumbo-Jumbo will hoo-doo you."

Part III, "The Hope of Their Religion," opens in a black American church, then shifts to the Congo. An old Negro minister urges his parishoners (mostly bums and prostitutes) to reform. All the energy of the earlier scense is present in the revival service. The preacher beats on the Bible so vigorously he wears it out. The drunken revelry, war dance, and minstrel show are transformed into a "jubilee revival shout." Some have visions and stand on chairs. The scene is wild. A thousand repent their "stupor and savagery and sin and wrong."

This, then, is the basis for Lindsay's vision and hope for salvation of the "Negro race" in Africa and America. Through Christianity and the revival service, with its many conversions, he imagines a race transformed from savagery to civilization, a people westernized and Christianized. Then he imagines the gray sky opening up like a "new-rent veil." The twelve apostles appear, clad in coats of mail, as Christian knights who will do battle with the witch-men and all other "demons." The apostles fill the forests with their heavenly cry. A "Congo paradise" is created in the ruins of the heathen, Mumbo-Jumbo culture. Even the thick jungle lands are defoliated and cleared for the "new creation." The new paradise is safe for babes at play, for the building of "temples clean," and "Mumbo-Jumbo is dead in the jungle."

This, of course, is no static set of images of black experience. There is a fury of action throughout, culminating in the defeat of the witch-men by Lindsay's company of angels and in the conversion of the natives. Savagism has been defeated (at least for the time) and a "black paradise" has been created in Africa and America. Civilization and Christianity have triumphed; the Congo's new Christians have been blessed with the beneficence of western colonialism and the zeal of the Christian mission. Those elements of Congo life that might most be praised if the poem were in the natural mode — the beauty of the uncleared jungle, the freedom, spontaneity, chilklike happiness of the natives — have been excoriated and altered. Instead, Lindsay sees the people of "The Congo" as a sin-infested cult led by "skull-faced witch-men" who celebrate death, not life.

The deceased missionary, Brother Eldred, went to the Congo, after all, not to admire its primitivism, but to subdue and remake it. His was a willful voyage to the "heart of darkness." Eldred's death is raison d'être for the Gothic tone of this tale. His death must be avenged, and Lindsay's poem works out that revenge, building a scenario that joins it with Eldred's goal for a new Congo. Lindsay fleshed out this scenario with bits and pieces of black life gleaned from his reading about and limited experience with blacks.

The poem's great popularity with white readers probably stems more from its bold rhymes, overpowering rhythm, and its combination of certain stereotypes of blacks than from its missionary zeal. Lindsay's clichés of black character (fun-loving, loose-living, half-savage) may appeal to the desire of many whites for such racist images. But to many people the poem's most powerful and lasting image is neither of fun-loving black folk nor of their conversion; it is of Mumbo-Jumbo and his power to "hoo-doo you." The

poem ends on this note, for though Mumbo reputedly is
dead, the vulture still cries his fearful curse. It is this spirit,
based on an assumption that the primitive is evil and that
the Congo must be the source of all evil, that most fascinated
Lindsay.

Curiously, "The Congo" and "General William Booth"
haunted Vachel Lindsay for the rest of his life. He recited
"The Congo" for sixteen years on public lecture tours. He
practically made his living on the reputation of these two
poems and a few others. But shortly before his suicide he
began to refuse to recite them. From a prep school in North
Carolina he sent the following telegram to his wife:

THIS SCHOOL HERE PUT ON THE THUMBSCREWS
TILL I WAS READY TO SCREAM BECAUSE THEY
COULD NOT SWEAT THE CONGO OUT OF ME
TWO MORE SUCH PERSECUTIONS AND I AM A
GONER FOR SURE (410)

Finally, he wrote, " 'I simply can't bear it.... Put it on all
my contracts that I refuse hereafter to recite *Booth, The
Congo*, or any other poems I do not choose to recite' " (411).
Somewhat later he wrote to his wife, " 'I will *not* be a *slave* to
my yesterdays. I will *not*. I was born *creator* not a parrot...' "
(412). Yet he was a slave to these now worn-out poems of his
youth on which his popular reputation rested. Of them it
was "The Congo" — the most flamboyant and vaudevillian
of them all — that he seemed to object to most in his last
years. Dragged down by the oppressive burden and a rising
debt, Lindsay committed suicide on the night of December
4, 1931. With "savage" revenge, Mumbo-Jumbo, the God of
the Congo, hoo-dooed Vachel Lindsay.

Consider the irony of his suicide. He was a parrot, after
all; he collected all the white clichés of black life he could
find, blended them together, and then recited the stale lines
over and over, thousands of times, to those demanding white

audiences. The poem and Lindsay's career are a sad
commentary on the "poet who wanted to be popular."

EUGENE O'NEILL

"The Congo" lived on long after Lindsay's suicide, of
course, to become one of America's most popular and most
frequently anthologized narrative poems. Even greater
literary popularity and admiration came to this next
illustration of the savage mode in American letters, Eugene
O'Neill's *The Emperor Jones*. Although critics have given
much higher praise for literary achievement to O'Neill's
play than to Lindsay's poem, the two have much in common.
O'Neill's portrait of Emperor Brutus Jones begins on a
Caribbean island, but the reader soon is transported to the
shores of Lindsay's Congo, to the heart of darkest Africa.
O'Neill aquired many of his images of Africa and of black
character from the same popular sources, but he probably
drew some of them directly from "The Congo." Lindsay's
"skull-faced witch-men" also appear in *The Emperor Jones*
and help bring O'Neill's black Emperor to his defeat. The
strongest dramatic effect of "The Congo," the "Boomalay
Boomalay Boomalay Boom" of the tribal drums (which
Lindsay would beat out as he recited the poem), become the
central dramatic effect of O'Neill's play. Although O'Neill
credits a different source for the idea, the haunting and
frenzied beat of the congo drum gives power and dramatic
effect to these works and became a stock-in-trade expression
of the savage mode.

Despite their similar exploitation of the savage mode, the
two works come to quite opposite conclusions. Lindsay
narrates the death of the savage and the conversion of Africa
into a Christian and "civilized" society. O'Neill, on the other
hand, dramatizes the defeat of a black American by his
"savage" Congo ancestors. While Lindsay depicted the death

of the savage, O'Neill used the savage to defeat a black man who was trying to emulate the white world's model of success. Despite their differences, both works assume their audiences will take vicarious pleasure in the presence of the savage.

The opening of *The Emperor Jones,* on November 1, 1920, may be viewed as a monumental event in American theater. As O'Neill biographer Travis Bogard expresses it, that night catapulted O'Neill and the Provincetown Players "beyond any horizon they had envisioned."[21] The opening was greeted with wildly favorable reviews. Alexander Woollcott, writing in the *New York Times,* described the play as "an extraordinarily striking and dramatic study of panic fear."[22] Heywood Broun observed that it seemed "just about the most interesting play that has yet come from the most promising playwright in America."[23] Broun went on to praise Charles Gilpin, the black actor who played Brutus Jones: "Gilpin was great. It is a performance of heroic stature." The play literally was an overnight success. The next morning a long line of theatergoers waited to buy tickets, and a thousand subscriptions were sold during the first week.[24] Originally scheduled for a two-week engagement, *The Emperor Jones* ran for 490 performances in New York before going on the road.

Not only was the play popular with white theatergoers and the hit of the season, it is regarded a "breakthrough" play in American theater. In addition to being boldly innovative in its staging techniques, *The Emperor Jones* was the first American play to employ black actors and develop a major black portrait. O'Neill's black portraits in *Thirst* (1914, a collection of five one-act plays), *The Moon of the Caribbees* (1918), *The Dreamy Kid* (1919), and *All God's Chillun Got Wings* (1924) stand as evidence of a growing white interest in portraying black life, concurrent with the emergence of the Negro Renaissance of black self-awareness and artistic expression. Despite this new interest in dramatizing black life, hardly any black actors were cast in black parts. Even O'Neill's earlier productions, *Thirst* and *Caribbees*, employed white actors in black face. Thus, *The Emperor Jones* holds a very special place in black American theater. In her study of Negro playwrights, Doris Abramson comments that O'Neill's plays and Paul Green's *In Abraham's Bosom* deserve credit for thrusting dramatizations of black life beyond the level of the minstrel show.[25] In his biography of O'Neill Travis Bogard comments that the play proved that a black figure and "an ordinary American could become a subject of pathetic concern and on occasion could rise to the height of a tragic figure." He expresses the judgment of a fair number of critics in saying that "American theater came of age with this play."[26] Although there is some truth to such statements, O'Neill's play deserves reevaluation in the context of the Harlem Renaissance and the "New Negro" movement. In this context O'Neill's portrait of Brutus Jones will be seen as another expression of the savage mode, incorporating several well-established white stereotypes of black character.

By the time *Jones* opened at the Provincetown Playhouse, Harlem was the largest black community in the world. It had already grown its own sizeable class of artists and well-educated residents. At the heart of the Harlem Renaissance was a serious effort on the part of black artists to interpret black life on its own terms. To be sure, works like *Jones* and Waldo Frank's *Holiday* (1923), Sherwood Anderson's *Dark Laughter* (1925), and Carl Van Vechten's *Nigger Heaven* (1926) provided encouragement to black writers, and, as Robert Bone puts it, they "created a sympathetic audience for the serious treatment of Negro subjects."[27] This interest among white writers in a literature of black experience also led to frequent patronage and sponsorship of black writers.[28] What has been largely overlooked is that this was a two-way process. White writers drew their materials and inspiration from the Renaissance, including the great burst of interest in Africana, and often at great expense to black life. The "New

Negro" movement was both a celebration of black achievement and a declaration of freedom from the white myths, melodramas, and stereotypes that characterized the "Old Negro." In the introduction to his celebrated anthology of a decade of black writing, *The New Negro* (1926), Alain Locke declared: "The popular melodrama has about played itself out, and it is time to scrap the fictions, garret the bogeys and settle down to a realistic facing of facts. The day of 'aunties,' and 'uncles' and 'mammies' is equally gone. Uncle Tom and Sambo have passed on."[29] Regrettably, Locke's assessment was too optimistic. *The Emperor Jones* itself is an example of the way in which old racial clichés and myths have been perpetuated, even in highly regarded literture.

Despite the new consciousness that was growing in and around Harlem and the call for greater sensitivity and realism in portraits of black life, O'Neill drew his black material from exotic settings and "Old Negro" sources. In 1909 he traveled to the rain forests of Honduras on a prospecting adventure. According to Travis Bogard, he was haunted by the presence of the jungle, and "he claimed that the pulse of blood in his eardrums during a bout with malaria on the trip gave him the idea of the drumbeat used throughout the play."[30] Both O'Neill and Vachel Lindsay were influenced by Africana such as Stanley's *In Darkest Africa* and Charles Sheeler's *African Negro Sculpture.*[31] It seems likely both had also read Conrad's *The Heart of Darkness*, with its depiction of the primordial darkness. Yet neither Lindsay nor O'Neill lifts his work to the level of Conrad's conclusion that savagery can reside in the hearts of *all* men.

A more detailed account of the drumbeat idea for the play comes from O'Neill's biographer Corswell Bowen. She quotes O'Neill as saying: " 'One day I was reading of the religious feasts in the Congo and the uses to which the drum was put there — how it starts at a normal pulse and is slowly accelerated until the heartbeat of everyone present corresponds to the frenzied beat of the drum. Here was the idea of an experiment. How could this sort of thing work on an audience in a theater?' "[32] The idea of the magic silver bullet came to O'Neill from a black circus employee. He told O'Neill the story of Vilbrun Guillaume Sam, who became dictator of Haiti and held onto his position for about six months. President Sam boasted, according to the version O'Neill heard, " 'They'll never get me with a lead bullet. I'll kill myself with a silver bullet first. Only a silver bullet can kill me.' "[33] From these sources and perhaps others O'Neill hit upon the two staggering effects of his play: the terrifying presence of the jungle and the increasing tempo of the tribal drumbeat.

It is also generally well known that O'Neill waged and finally won an energetic campaign to get Charles Gilpin, who played Brutus Jones superbly, reinvited to the annual New York Drama League dinner of 1920. The original invitation had been withdrawn when members of the League protested at being asked to dine with a Negro. O'Neill was furious and exerted such pressure on the League that they reinvited the black actor. Yet the O'Neill who championed Gilpin on that occasion showed a very different attitude at another time. Gilpin, obviously unhappy with certain aspects of his role, made several changes in the script, including a substitution of "black baby" for O'Neill's "nigger." When O'Neill discovered this he told Gilpin, " 'If I ever catch you rewriting my lines again, you black bastard, I'm going to beat you up.' "[34] These two incidents are characteristic of O'Neill's racial ambivalence. He could defend Gilpin against segregation yet call him a "black bastard" for deleting "nigger" from the script. He created a role that established the careers of Charles Gilpin and Paul Robeson, yet approached his black portraits with insensitivity and maladroitness, consequently perpetuating pejorative images of black life.

As the play opens, Brutus Jones, after fleeing from the

United States, has established himself within two years as emperor of a small island in the West Indies. Life has become so pleasant that he has almost forgotten the possibility of white intervention or of a native revolt. In rising to his position of wealth and power Jones has exhibited those qualities of free-enterprise leadership he has assimilated from successful whites during his ten years as a pullman car porter: shrewdness, aggressiveness, self-reliance, strength of will.

Yet O'Neill undercuts his reasonably attractive and heroic portrait of a black adventurer with derisively conventional, stereotypic images of blacks as savages. Consider the playwright's opening description of his protagonist:

> Jones enters from the right. He is a tall, powerfully-built, full-blooded negro of middle age. His features are typically negroid, yet there is something decidedly distinctive about his face — an underlying strength of will, a hardy, self-reliant confidence in himself that inspires respect. His eyes are alive with a keen, cunning intelligence. In manner he is shrewd, suspicious, evasive. He wears a light-blue uniform coat, sprayed with brass buttons, heavy gold chevrons on his shoulders, gold braid on his collar, cuffs, etc. His pants are bright red, with a light-blue stripe down the side. Patent leather laced boots with brass spurs, and a belt with a long-barreled, pearl-handled revolver in a holster, complete his make-up. Yet there is something not altogether ridiculous about his grandeur. He has a way of carrying it off.[35]

The words "yet" and "not altogether ridiculous" reveal O'Neill's essential attitude toward Jones. The emperor has certain "distinctive" qualities despite his "typically negroid" features. His dress is perhaps "not altogether," but mostly "ridiculous."

Even though O'Neill establishes Jones as an individual with a particular past and a distinct personality, the tone of his portrait is pejorative. The Emperor Jones is more clown than hero, ultimately a laughable pretender to be pitied and dismissed. O'Neill's bias reveals itself as the play progresses, presenting the defeat not of white colonialism and free enterprise, as some critcs would have it, but of an "uppity" black man who presumed to model himself after successful white exploiters. The revenge of the play is complete as Jones reverts to a savage and is defeated, then killed by his own people.

When he discovers a rebellion is in the making Jones leaves his palace swiftly and reaches with ease the margin of the primitive landscape, the great forest. Having studied the methods of white colonialists, he has made elaborate plans for just such an emergency, stashing away a supply of food and memorizing the trails through the forest. He also knows where to meet a French gunboat that will take him to Martinique and to the fortune in taxes he has extracted from his subjects.

It quickly becomes clear that Jones is his own worst enemy, defeating himself in the jungle of his own irrationality even before the natives begin to hunt him. Although prepared to penetrate the actual jungle before his pursuers mobilize, he is ill-equipped to venture into the jungle of his mind. O'Neill has allowed Jones to succeed temporarily by imitating what he has learned from white colonialism and capitalism. Once under the pressure of pursuit, however, this modern black hero quickly disintegrates to his former tribal identity. Like the black people in Vachel Lindsay's "The Congo," he is terrified that he will encounter "skull-faced, lean witch-doctors," and "tattooed cannibals" with "voo-doo rattles."

For a while the forces opposing him are kept at a distance. In scene two, Brutus can find neither his food cache nor the trail he has marked, and this begins to unnerve him. It is the "formless fears," manifestations of his own growing fear and guilt, that he cannot tolerate. In reaction he fires the first of his six bullets. Scenes three and four reinforce the feeling that one is being conducted through the jungle of a man's mind in storm. In these hallucinatory episodes Brutus imagines that he meets first Jeff, the black man who died of razor wounds he inflicted, then the prison gang and the white guard he killed. If a man is plagued and tormented by his own past and his unconscious, how can he expect to cope with his conscious mind and external reality?

In the first four scenes O'Neill has employed techniques that appear in many of his plays. The first of these is the retrograde movement of Jones away from crisis and from life itself. As Eugene Waith comments, "The backward movement of O'Neill characters is always flight from the problems posed by existence; forward movement is the heroic, sometimes ecstatic, acceptance of them."[36] The second technique, as John Gassner puts it, is O'Neill's "response to the vogue of depth psychology through which he attempts to dramatize subconscious tensions."[37] With scene five he adds to these a third dimension, based on the general concept known as atavism. Atavism stems from the two general postulates that some individuals exhibit traits and character-istics of ancestors, absent in intervening generations, and that individuals occasionally revert to the features and life styles of their ancestors.

This fifth scene is crucial to an understanding of the play. In the three previous incidents Brutus Jones has faced images from his own past. So far it has been possible to believe that O'Neill is presenting an *Inferno*-like trip through Jones's personal past. The hallucinations can even be explained as resulting from Jones's extreme hunger:

> Sho'! Dat was all in yo' own head. Wasn't nothin' there! Wasn't no Jeff! Know what? Yo' jus' get seein' dem thing 'cause yo' belly's empty an' you's sick wid hunger inside. Hunger 'fects yo' head an' yo' eyes. Any fool know dat. (38)

With scene five, however, O'Neill moves from Jones's

personal to his racial past. He has long since lost his emperor's costume; he is barefooted now and clad in a loin cloth, his body scratched and bruised. He has already cast off the trappings of royalty: the light-blue jacket with its gold chevrons and braid, the patent leather boots, the brass spurs. Terrified by the last encounter, Brutus collapses beside a stump, overcome by feelings of guilt over the deaths of Jeff and the prison guard. "Lawd, I done wrong!... Forgive me, Lawd! Forgive dis po' sinner! (*then beseeching terrifiedly*) An' keep dem away, Lawd! Keep dem away from me! An' stop dat drum soundin' in my ears! Dat begin to sound ha'nted, too" (42).

He rises from this prayer imagining he is in the midst of a slave auction; a group of white Southern ladies and gentlemen are looking at him admiringly, prepared to bid handsomely. Brutus watches the pantomime before him, the auctioneer's silent spiel, the planters raising their fingers in bidding. "*Convulsed with raging hatred and fear*," Brutus shouts, "Is dis a auction?" Is yo' sellin' me like dey uster befo' de war?...I shows you I'se a free nigger, damn yo' souls!" (44-45). He fires at the auctioneer and the planter. With the shots the walls of the forest close in on the auction, and Jones, crying out, rushes headlong into the forest.

With scene six Jones finds himself inside the hold of a slave ship. He has receded further back in racial time, and — as with the slave auction — beyond the experiential level of his own existence. He is moving back through the history of slavery. Shackled with other slaves to the walls of the vessel, Jones is at first terrified by his new circumstance, throwing himself to the deck to "shut out the sight." But he soon resigns himself and joins them in their wail of despair. "His voice, as if under some uncanny compulsion, starts with the others. As their chorus lifts he rises to a sitting posture similar to the others, swaying back and forth. His voice reaches the highest pitch of sorrow, of desolation" (47).

The last of the hallucinatory scenes finds Jones, by now a

stone-faced shell of a man, before his ancestral and racial birthplace, and presumably on the shores of the Congo. There is nothing overtly terrifying about the setting: it is quiet; he is alone. Jones sinks before the stone altar, kneeling in devotion to its unknown deity, "as if in obedience to some obscure impulse." Then Brutus catches hold of himself, shocked by his own obeisance before a pagan altar, and cries for help from his Christian god. He tries to resist the pagan cult but is so thoroughly hypnotized by its ritual dance and the gestures of the witch-doctor that even his resistance becomes feigned, as a pantomime expressing flight and pursuit.

> Jones has become completely hypnotized. His voice joins in the incantation, in the cries; he beats time with his hands and sways his body to and fro from the waist. The whole spirit and meaning of the dance has entered into him, has become his spirit. (49)

O'Neill has been preparing his audience for this culminating scene from the moment Jones entered the jungle — and even before. From momentary harmony with his racial past, Jones realizes — in horror — the intent of the frenzied dancing: "The forces of evil demand sacrifice. They must be appeased. . . . Jones seems to sense the meaning of this. It is he who must offer himself for sacrifice" (49-50). Despite fervent prayers, he receives no help from the Christian god. Although Jones survives the scene it is a pyrrhic victory, for he has had to fire his silver bullet at the crocodile god. He emerges from the depths of the forest a defeated ruin of a man and is shot by his pursuers with a silver bullet.

Edwin Engle sees *The Hairy Ape*, rather than *The Emperor Jones*, as O'Neill's fullest exploration of primitivism and atavism. O'Neill himself characterized Yank as "a symbol of a man who has lost that old harmony with nature, the harmony which he used to have as an animal and has not acquired in a spiritual way."[38] In fact, none of O'Neill's heroes finds easy sanctuary or salvation; if not terrified by emanations from their own pasts, they are brutalized by the economic and industrial forces of the present. Characteristically, O'Neill's heroes live in a perilous state, either enslaved or suffering a loss of vitality. Engle indicates O'Neill's debt to Jack London and Frank Norris in the use of the ancestral past. Both explored in their novels the "theme of the persistence in modern man of the brutish cave man" in which a disassociation of personality results from the conflict between the hero and his primordial ancestry.[39]

The particular thrust of *The Emperor Jones,* however, is in the direction of a black atavism. It exploits those stereotypes in the white imagination which associate blacks with the savage and a jungle landscape. It is as if O'Neill were saying that the argument for *black* atavism is more plausible because of the black man's more recent, jungle past. Jones's thin surface of reason crumbles before the great, seething maelstrom of his fears, "ha'nts," apparitions, and the call of his pagan religion. It surges through his blood. The beat of the tom-tom is the beat of his savage heart, the drumbeat stopping at the instant of his death. The modern black man is a walking savage thinly disguised by western culture and religion; he is his own greatest enemy — or so the play would have it.

Thus can one begin to see the extent of O'Neill's indulgence in the savage mode. But in addition to the savage, Brutus Jones embodies some of the oldest and most loathsome white stereotypes of black character. The opening scene describes the gaudy, somewhat absurd, although "not *altogether* ridiculous" [*my* italics] costume that Jones wears. His name has about it a comic suggestiveness as well: Brutus the Brute. It is not unlike the name suggestion of Babo (baboon) in *Benito Cereno.* By invoking that vein of white humor regarding elaboration and pretention in black names (Emperor Brutus Jones), O'Neill establishes a mock-serious tone from the start, and puts Jones's position as emperor in comic jeopardy.[40] The gaudy facade of the palace, pillars, and throne, and the absence of subjects, only add to this atmosphere. In the jungle he becomes a Sambo figure; his "eyes pop out" and he is too scared to run. The defeat of Jones is the defeat of a black pretender and not of the white entrepreneurs and exploiters he emulated. Brutus Jones never had a chance in *The Emperor Jones*.

In his autobiography *The Big Sea*, Langston Hughes describes the disastrous and abbreviated run of *The Emperor Jones* in Harlem:

> Somewhat later, I recall a sincere but unfortunate attempt on Jules Bledsoe's part to bring "Art" to Harlem. He appeared in Eugene O'Neill's *The Emperor Jones* at the old Lincoln Theater on 135th Street, a theater that had, for all its noble name, been devoted largely to ribald, but highly entertaining, vaudeville of the "Butterbeans and Susie" type. The audience didn't know what to make of *The Emperor Jones* on a stage where "Shake That Thing" was formerly the rage. And when the Emperor started running naked through the forest, hearing the Little Frightened Fears, naturally they howled with laughter.
>
> "Them ain't no ghosts, fool!" the spectators cried from the orchestra. "Why don't you come on out o' that jungle — back to Harlem where you belong?"
>
> In the manner of Stokowski hearing a cough at the Academy of Music, Jules Bledsoe stopped dead in his tracks, advanced to the footlights, and proceeded to lecture his audience on manners in the theater. But the audience wanted none of *The Emperor Jones*. And their manners had been all right at all the other shows at the Lincoln, where they took part in the performances at will. So when Brutus continued his flight, the audience again howled with laughter. And that was the end of *The Emperor Jones* on 135th Street.[41]

Although O'Neill's Harlem audience probably knew little, intellectually, of psychic journeys and the racial unconscious, they felt that the jungle had no connection with their lives, and they recognized the stereotypes that O'Neill was using.

One can share their amusement and annoyance. Their response is profoundly revealing, for it hints at how often whites have written to satisfy their own needs and at how they have stereotyped and distorted black life in doing so.

Other voices in Harlem during the Renaissance expressed their growing objection to counterfeit portraits of black life. Black critics writing in journals such as *Dial, Opportunity, Crisis, Outlook,* and *Independent,* assessed portraits of black life produced by white and black writers alike. Writing for *Crisis,* Benjamin Brawley commented that well-intentioned white writers such as O'Neill, Ridgley Torrence (*Granny Maumee*), and Ernest Culbertson (*Goat Alley*) apparently portrayed blacks as primitives because their cultural blinders limited them to a conception of blacks as "inferior, superstitious, half-ignorant." Such writers, he continued, could not begin to render the "immense paradox of racial life."[42] Toward the end of the decade further resistance to white images of black life began to be heard. *Crisis,* for example, ran a five-issue symposium on how black people ought to be depicted in American literature.[43] George C. Morse summarizes much of the objection to primitive portraits and voodooism in fiction by commenting, "they are legion who believe that if a native band from the jungles of Africa should parade the streets beating their tom-toms, all the black inhabitants of our city would lose their acquired dignity and dance to its rhythm by virtue of inheritance alone."[44]

George Morse's comments read as if directed to *The Emperor Jones.* Even though O'Neill was attempting to revive tragedy and to dramatize the self-destructiveness of the lust for power, the details of his play allow no such universality of theme. The stereotypes of black character are too blatant to be overlooked. The retrograde movement of the play encompasses black history and thereby carries with it implied racial statements. In addition to the accusation of inherent atavism, the play is a defeat not of capitalism and colonialism but of blacks who aspire to such goals.

Ironically, the excellent acting of the black actors Gilpin and Robeson and the theatrical effects O'Neill gleaned from his superficial contacts with black life combined to produce a play that, along with a few others by O'Neill, "shaped the course of American Drama in its most significant developmental period, from 1915 to about 1930."[45] Nor did *The Emperor Jones* die in the succeeding decades as an antiquated and pejorative portrait of a black man. DuBose Heyward, author of *Porgy*, wrote the scenario for the film version of *Jones*, which also starred Paul Robeson. Louis Greenberg's operatic version of the play opened at the Metropolitan Opera in January 1933, with Lawrence Tibbett as Jones (58-59).

How is one to account for this popularity, even into the present time? To be sure, the play incorporated stunning effects, strengthened by excellent black acting. Yet black critics and audiences were able to see the stereotypes and the put-down that thrilled white audiences: the "civilized terror in the presence of the savage," as Pearce so aptly phrased it. Had O'Neill been less interested in dramatic effects, less swayed by racial stereotypes, he could have written authentic tragedy in which Brutus Jones came to the recognition that he had exploited and underestimated the skill of his own people. Instead, O'Neill gives the last lines to the cockney Smithers, establishing beyond all doubt the play's racial bias. Smithers dismisses Jones and his assassins with contemptuous scorn. "Stupid as 'ogs, the lot of 'em! Blarstered niggers!"

WALDO FRANK

Waldo Frank's novel *Holiday* (1923) serves both as the fourth illustration of the savage mode and as a transition to portraiture in the natural mode of expression. As with

Stephen Crane in "The Monster," Frank attempts to maintain an ironic distinction between elements of "the savage" the white community in his novel projects onto his black protagonist, John Cloud, and the reality of the man's life. Frank carries this bifurcated racial consciousness much further than Crane and maintains his distinction between savage thinking and racial reality much more successfully. He clearly approaches "the savage" as a white obsession that is destructive to both races. Unlike Lindsay and O'Neill, Frank maintains sufficient distance from both races to explore the savage mode without being consumed by it. This stance allows him to present more accurate and life-like black portraits than would have otherwise been possible. Waldo Frank's association with the black writer Jean Toomer, and their travels through the south together as he prepared himself to write *Holiday*, is in itself a fascinating story of a white writer's growth in racial consciousness and largely explains the complexity of his fictional approach to black life.

Frank was indebted to Toomer for his unusually sensitive rendering of black character. In early 1921, and again in the fall of 1922, Frank and Toomer traveled together through the South. Frank commented in his notebook that Toomer coached him in the nuances of black dialect. According to biographer, Paul Carter, the two traveled through Virginia, South Carolina, Alabama, Mississippi, and Louisiana, and Frank "posed as a Negro in order to avoid incidents while he tried to feel with these exiles from American civilization. He rode in Jim Crow coaches, lived with Toomer's friends, spoke in a Negro church on science and religion."[46] As Frank expresses it in his memoirs, "No question would be asked about my race; it would be quietly assumed that if I came with Toomer I must be a Negro."[47] Frank observes that this was not madness, since he had seen many Negroes who were "more white than I."

The remarkable opportunity Toomer provided for Frank

as a white writer was "a chance to see and feel the Negro from
within the inside angle of the Negro." As the trip continued
Frank identified more and more strongly with the situation
and outlook of the black people he visited. He comments, "I
felt *with* the Negro. This empathy was startling. Lying in
dark sleep I would dream I was a Negro, would spring from
sleep reaching for my clothes on the chair beside my bed, to
finger them, to smell them, . . .in proof I was white and
myself."[48] Frank may also have discovered the limits of his
ability to extend his brotherhood and identify with the black
world he was exploring. During the trip he discovered a
mutual resentment, if not hatred, among the two races. The
whites resented the seeming happiness, the laughter and
song, the carefree attitudes of the blacks. Conversely, the
blacks laughed to cover up their hatred, and they practiced
"Christian charity as an act of self-preservation against their
self-destroying hatred."[49] Through Toomer he came to see
black music and dance as both mask and means of survival in
a hostile environment. Frank returned from the trip inspired,
and completed the first draft of the novel *Holiday* within the
next month.

Although Waldo Frank was a prodigious writer (fourteen
novels, eighteen social histories, scores of articles) and
widely known in the twenties, he has, perhaps unjustly,
received very limited attention since then. Critical bio-
graphies of Frank have dealt with his novels in summary
fashion, without detailed examination of *Holiday* and its
handling of black character.

Frank's ideas about western civilization and about his
function as a writer and critic should prove helpful to an
understanding of *Holiday*. One of Frank's fullest presentations
of his ideas is contained in *Our America*.[50] Here he states his
conviction that western civilization has been dying since the
Renaissance, its grand heritage strangling in materialism.
He sees contemporary life unwholesomely fragmented and
spiritually wounded. The hope for America and the West

lies in reviving the spiritual values found at high points in the Judeo-Christian tradition. Frank is openly hostile to the machine, modern science, and empirical rationalism, his objection lying chiefly in their disregard for intuition. In opposition to the alien forces about him, Frank promulgates a philosophy of "organic wholeness," in which the individual purifies himself of selfishness and egocentricity. Transformed by his new awareness of cosmic totality and unity, the individual accepts life and finds love in all things. Most of Frank's novels depict this process of the death of self and birth of the "Person." As Frank expressed it,

> We must break our important habit of constant issuance into petty deed... We must begin to generate within ourselves the energy which is love of life. For that energy, to whatever form the mind consign it, is religious. Its act is creation.[51]

Waldo Frank has no lofty notions about the pioneering phase of American settlement. It was to him a repressive process, devoid of spiritual richness, in which every narrowing instinct of self-preservation and acquisition tended to make the pioneers intolerant, materialistic, unaesthetic. The legacy from this period is one of power and greed, Frank argues; there was no richness of values to be found in taming the wilderness. "Materialism," he wrote, "was an invisible magnet toward which each element of New England thought and life needed to point."[52]

In short, Waldo Frank sees a terrible sickness plaguing American life. Some of the remedies he envisions have their sources in earlier societies while others come from aspects of black life in America. Frank's predilection to cultural primitivism leads him to observe that while many whites would regard the "Alabama Negro" as an "illiterate, often drunk, rather vulgar creature," such conclusions are unjustified: "In his native state, he [the Alabama Negro] draws from the soil and the sky, in whose cycles he is seasoned, a grace which is refined even if it be unconscious, like the grace of a flower."[53]

As is typical of writers attracted to the natural mode of primitivism, Frank attempts to correct white prejudice and stereotyping, but in so doing he simplifies and romanticizes black life. In his novel *Holiday* Frank posits his cultural primitivism (which bestows on blacks the natural "grace of a flower") against the conviction of his white characters that beneath their seeming docility black males are a constant threat to white southern women. Unfortunately, the novel is flawed by a melodramatic plot, cumbersome symbolism, and a ponderous style. Still, the work does not deserve its literary oblivion, if for no other reason than its complex racial understanding.

Miss Virginia Slade and the other whites of *Holiday* live in Nazareth, an ugly little town on the Gulf of Mexico. John Cloud, the black foreman at the Slade's fruit farm, lives in one of the "paintless shanties of Niggertown." He is torn by a conflict between his dreams and the reality of his life. Race relations in Nazareth are distant and orderly, for blacks know the white man's codes and dare not break them. John is recognized by whites as a man of leadership, but he is despised for his boldness. He has dared to look a white woman — Virginia Slade — full in the face and to watch the motions of her body as she walked down the street. John Cloud is, as his name suggests, a free spirit, not to be confined by convention or code.

In one of the most illuminating scenes of this novel, John sits down at the edge of a cotton field. He picks up a cotton boll, holds it lovingly, but then notices that a weevil is eating away at it from the inside. The more he considers this common event the more he sees it as a miniature of his own life. The lovely cotton boll is analogous to the plight of black people. Both were brought here for the white man's profit. Although the surface of the boll seems undisturbed, the weevil is there like a cancer; it destroys from within. The weevil is to the boll as the white man and his racial caste system are to black people. John extracts the weevil from the cotton boll.

> The dirty little spot within his palm and thumb stands against the sweep of the whole world. Its tiny hardness, its dissonant prick in his flesh are like his thought that bites upon his view. John wavers in the alien sense of a weevil pricking his skin, and a thought, his sight.[54]

The weevil, drawing blood, foreshadows John's death by white hands. Frank wants his reader to see that the weevil is both the whites of Nazareth and the whole repressive culture John Cloud lives in.

John's mother fears he will become like her brother Wallace, who was forced to flee from Nazareth.

> My brother Wallace, He had a dream lak you. What was it? . . . Jus a dream of a black man's breathin' free. An' 'se dream give a look to his eyes . . . . He was lookin' at air: at free open sky. (22)

Mrs. Cloud would far prefer her son abandon his dream than lose him to a white man's vengeance.

Virginia Slade is both sexually frustrated and something of a cultural primitivist. She yearns for the simplicity and happiness that she thinks the blacks who work for her possess. At times she even yearns to be reborn so that she might have the seeming naturalness and spontaneity of their lives. At night she lies in bed, sleepless and tormented by sexual desire for John and the pain she imagines to be her dying soul. She lays her body and soul open to the night, thinking, "Night, you're a raping Nigger!" In a moment of fantasy she imagines her soul is black, though her skin stays white. Against the vitality she sees in black life, Virginia places the decadence and ossification of her white culture.

Virginia's fantasy that black men are sexual savages is

echoed in a poem Claude McKay reprinted in his autobiography, *A Long Way From Home*.[55] The poem was written
by "a certain young Southern white lady," as she called
herself, who describes her visit to Harlem:

Temptation

I couldn't forget
The banjo's whang
And the piano's bang
As we strutted the do-do-do's
In Harlem!

That pansy sea!
A tossing me
All loose and free, O, lily me!
In muscled arms
Of ebony.

I couln't forget
That black boy's eyes
That black boy's shake
That black boy's size
I couldn't forget
O, snow white me!

The sexual aspects of the savage mode that Frank is
exploring in *Holiday* are evident in this poem. The young
southern white lady in the poem imagines her Harlem
partner to be a black Eros. Her recollection of the excursion
is a curious fusion of sentimentality and eroticism. She is
presumably expressing the stereotype of blacks as sexual
savages that her white culture has taught her. It is also
possible that the poem is really a dream-like wish fulfillment.
No doubt her trip to Harlem would have been forbidden by
her family. Much of the pleasure of the adventure comes
from its naughtiness, for she seems both attracted to the
black man and frightened by him. This ambivalence of

tangled emotions is a variation on the nightmare and dream pattern that goes hand in glove with the savage and natural modes of primitivism. Occasionally these two emotional responses by whites to blacks coexist, as in "Temptation," and in *Holiday*. Aspects of this ambivalence are also present in "The Congo" and "The Monster."

Either in fact or in fancy, this white adventuress has been transported to Harlem, that never-never land; she dances and whirls as if on a "pansy sea." It is a fairy-tale voyage to a land where the beautiful and the frightening occur simultaneously. The "pansy sea" of "Temptation" is also a sea of racial color, of faces of color. The young lady admits to becoming "all loose and free" — free from her inhibition and custom. Like Virginia Slade, she is free, perhaps for the first time, to express long-repressed desires. She remembers the boldness of the music and the permissiveness of Harlem, where one strutted the "do-do-do's" and forgot about the "don'ts." She also does not forget "the black boy's eyes," his shake, his size. The poem is not an exposition of a particular black man or really of Harlem but of the mind of a white woman, a woman who probably craved greater freedom than her culture allowed, who was sexually frustrated and desired what she had been denied: the possibility of a black friend or lover. The naughtiness of the adventure is established through the title and the contrast between his muscled blackness and her flower-like fragility and snowy whiteness.

Waldo Frank develops a similar pattern of contrasts between the two races and cultures in *Holiday*. Miss Slade, like her counterpart in "Temptation," rejects her restrictive, repressive white culture and enters the black countryside in search of adventure. The specific occasion for Virginia's rebellion and flight from Nazareth is revival week in the white community. The emotional tyranny of revivalism is emblematic of the larger tyranny of Southern white culture in the novel. While the Nazarenes flock to their revival tent,

Virginia sets out to roam the countryside and to look for
John. For Virginia, the revival tent is

> loathsome white: a small mucilaginous sack holding
> a spider's eggs...myriad black live spots that crawl, that
> will spread — let me out! (121)

Her image of spiders is not too distant from John Cloud's
image of the white man as boll weevil. To Virginia, the
spider is loathsome and vile, perhaps even as destructive as
the weevil is to John. Their choice of images reflects their
similar craving for freedom — but also the vast dissimilarity
of their situations.

Virginia walks from Nazareth to Niggertown. She is drawn
toward the settlement, not understanding exactly why, but
thinking. "O you have so much! Low down...." As she
walks her thoughts become clearer. Black people should pity
her and her pale face with its deceptions, its lies, for it cannot
see the blazing ease and the simple truth of the black race.
Yes, they should pity the white man, she thinks. "I'll not feel
sorry for you blazing niggers. You grow out of the soil.
Your flesh stays sweet in the dark flames of the South."

> When you sing and play, you forget us.
> Our play does not forget you.
> When you plow and sow, you forget us.
> Our hunger does not forget you. (143)

As Virginia's pilgrimage progresses, her imagination gen-
erates fantasies further and further from the realities of black
life. The black community, its cabins squalid along the dusty
road and shaded by chinaberry trees, gives her a "sense of
faëry." The cabins seem to her like painted toys and "the
nigger world is a music filling the world from the trees right
down to the earth."[56] But Virginia does not detect the
"resentment, already old" on the faces of the black children

who stare at her as she approaches. She cannot see the silent hatred of the community still grieving over the loss of one of its brothers, a stevedore who fell into the water while unloading the steamer *Psyche* at the Nazareth town pier. Several white men who knew how to swim watched him drown; none were willing to get their white flannels soaked to save a "nigger."

The second point about this scene is that although Virginia does not notice the black resentment, Waldo Frank does. The drowning yesterday, and now the looks of anguish and hatred on the children's faces, stand in grim irony against Virginia's "sense of faëry." Frank deliberately and effectively juxtaposes the simplicity and happiness Virginia imagines to exist with the tension and complexity of life in the black community. Virginia holds the simplistic and naive perspective of a cultural primitivist.

Somewhat earlier, John Cloud has left the black settlement and hiked to a spot on a bluff overlooking the Gulf. It is a location he frequents often, but no white men and few blacks venture here:

No hand is here. No white palm has scooped this fairness into possessive drought. All is wide, all is free. The sun is a free dance in the Heaven: earth and water rest sweetly in John's mind, his own...their lovely breadth...balming the stars of his soul. (138)

The white man, like the boll weevil, is to John a continual and malign presence. John needs to retreat from white civilization to find peace and momentary unity with the world. Stripping off his clothing, he dives from the rocky bluff into the Gulf. He emerges and climbs back to his promontory, feeling alive again, "like a young tree" thrusting up from the soil.

But nature offers no special protection for blacks in *Holiday.* John's solitude is shattered by his sudden realization that he is standing nude before Virginia Slade. She has watched his fine, bronzed body knife into the water and swim with ease and beauty. He retreats to find his clothing. She is, after all, a threat to his life. Even to be found in the woods with a white woman is considered adequate cause for lynching a black man in the world of *Holiday*. But after dressing he returns to Virginia. They talk for a while, even hold hands and look at each other with desire. Virginia tells him she also desires to swim and "to lie naked, to run naked in the world." Just watching John has given her ease. But now she wants to have sex with him. At least he could do that, she thinks; he could plant life in her to make her free.

John is thoroughly frightened by her suggestions and advances. But at her insistence he unwittingly exchanges pocket knives with her and then leaves. Even though he has refused her, Virginia has his knife. She holds the blade "like a tongue before her," then plunges it into her "waist." As she stabs herself, Virginia cries out, "Nigger! I am your world. You cannot break with me."

After the exchange of knives but before he leaves Virginia, John has had the same subconscious thought: "I am John Cloud, Nigger." He rejects Virginia because he is neither a black Eros nor the natural man she wishes him to be. For one, he is happily engaged to a black woman. But he also cannot afford to forget he is a black man in the white South and is therefore more repressed and inhibited than Virginia can imagine. While he may have some sexual desire for Virginia, he is certainly unwilling to trade his life for sex with a white woman. He has no secret powers; the woods will not harbor him. Clearly this is not the midsummer's dream Virginia fantasized.

Yet John cannot break with Virginia, as she has warned him. The exchange of knives is a fatal mistake. The wound she has inflicted upon herself is at best cumbersome symbolism. It is partially her attempt, as Paul Carter has suggested, to cut herself off from the black world that has rejected her, and it is symbolic sexual intercourse. But the act may also be seen as a double punishment: Virginia punishes herself for misjudging John and black people in general; she also punishes John for rejecting her and for refusing to play the role she expected of him.[57] Yet she has come to the painful discovery that "her" blacks do not live the simple, primitive lives she had romantically assumed.

John's death comes quickly. When Virginia is seen in town, bloodied and clutching a knife identified as John Cloud's, a lynch mob quickly forms. As the word spreads, the Nazarenes rush from their revival tent to get ropes and guns. John Cloud is brought back to Nazareth and lynched for a crime he did not commit. Frank describes the tragedy of *Holiday* this way:

> Here is a dual world, each part of which yearns in its racial way for self-expression, for joy, for life, for God: each part of which profoundly loves and needs what the other part possesses, and through the fateful circumstances of American life, all this energy of desire is locked into opposition and distrust so that it becomes channeled not in some fair communion but in orgy of blood and horror.[58]

Waldo Frank's comments here and elsewhere indicate he was interested, most of all, in illustrating two fractured, unrealized races. He echoes W.E.B. DuBois's *The Souls of Black Folk* when he says that each race "profoundly loves and needs what the other possesses." Frank was not, as he said, interested in taking sides in a racial dispute, nor did he intend to cast his characters as heroes or villains.

There is considerable discrepancy between these stated aims and the novel's achievement. Perhaps Frank did not wish to admit that he had created in John Cloud the image of a black Christ, but consider the evidence. His initials are J. C. He grows up and learns his trade in a town named Nazareth, becoming a leader of his people. He departs from civilization for the wilderness and there is tempted, sexually,

by the devil disguised as a white woman. He resists her
temptation, but on returning to civilization is betrayed,
abducted, and crucified. In this sense Virginia becomes both
devil and Judas. *Holiday* implies what Malcolm X says
directly in his autobiography; from his perspective the white
man *is* the devil. Cloud's tragic flaw is the moment of
weakness during which he agrees to exchange knives with
Virginia.

Seen from John Cloud's position, the whole framework of
the savage mode is reversed in *Holiday*. A white female
chases a black male. It is *The Clansman* in reverse. The web
Virginia weaves is Gothic in shape; her victim will either
submit to her desires and then be killed, or be killed for not
submitting.

Although *Holiday* is a novel with severe shortcomings in
character development, its significance is considerable. Frank's
detached point of view provides the needed distance from
the cultural primitivism of his white protagonist so that he
can develop the consciousness of his black protagonist as
well. Rarely does this occur among white writers. He also
shows sensitive awareness of and fully examines the very
different needs of both races. Blacks need freedom from
white oppression; whites need freedom from their own
oppressive culture. Of even greater importance, he illustrates
the destructiveness of cultural primitivism among whites
through its simplification of the complexities of black life
and its misjudgment of black character. Frank also shows
rich innovation on the usual patterns of the primitive modes
by fusing savagism and cultural primitivism. Much of
Frank's sensitivity to his subject undoubtedly stemmed from
his close friendship with Jean Toomer and from their trip
through the South together. This trip occurred while Frank
was planning and writing *Holiday* and Toomer was writing
the stories that make up his celebrated "novel," *Cane* (1923).
As Darwin Turner has pointed out in his study of Jean
Toomer (*In A Minor Chord* [1971]), Frank approached his

novel about black-white relationships with uncertainty and humility.[59] It was not until after his discussions with Toomer and his trip South to authenticate his ideas that he began writing *Holiday*. For these reasons Waldo Frank's *Holiday* is a significant achievement among the attempts of white writers to portray black life in America.

Contrary to the judgment of Nancy Tischler in her book *Black Masks* (1969), it seems most unlikely that the stereotyped "brute Negro" has disappeared from literature in recent times.[60] The black savage figure will remain, in fact, as long as whites continue to characterize blacks in some form of the savage modality and writers express or expose this tendency. Some examples from contemporary writing suggest that white writers continue to be drawn to this mode of characterization.

Tennessee Williams's *Sweet Bird of Youth* (1959) refers to castration of a young black man by a southern white mob.[61] Their innocent victim stands as warning to black men in the community to avoid all contact with white women. Williams dramatizes the sexual insecurity of the white males of the community as they project onto black men a super sexuality and fanatic interest in white women that the facts of the play do not substantiate. The symbolic castration, with all the hideous insecurity and envy it conveys, is even justified by the governor of the state as a warning that pollution of the white race will not be condoned.

Although not contained within either the savage or the natural strands of primitivism, William Styron's novel *The Confessions of Nat Turner* (1967) is an enormously important book in the dismal history of white attempts at depicting black character and life. Styron purports to document the 1831 slave revolt led by Nat Turner in Southampton, Virginia in which fifty-five whites were killed. Since almost nothing is known of Nat Turner's actual life, William Styron's protagonist is almost entirely a product of his own imagination and fantasies. Styron's Nat Turner appears as a thankless slave who leads an orgiastic murder of his basically decent and enlightened slave masters. Yet beneath his wanton and fearful savagery is revealed a black man who despises his fellow blacks, and although celibate and holding no desire for black women, dreams of copulating with a young white woman. Styron's Nat Turner is defeated and debased as surely as is O'Neill's Brutus Jones. Styron, however, is not confined to aspects of the savage but draws from the entire storehouse of racial stereotypes for his portrait. An extensive critical discussion of the novel is contained in *William Styron's Nat Turner: Ten Black Writers Respond* (1968).[62]

Francis Gaither's somewhat earlier novel *The Red Cock Crows* (1944) also portrays an obsession in the white South with the image of the black male as sexual savage. During one scene in Gaither's novel a white woman is reduced to hysteria and terror when a young black boy walks into her room. As if in ironic contrast to scenes like this, the black novelist Richard Wright portrays in *Native Son* (1940) a young black man so frightened by the prospect of being caught in a white girl's room that he accidentally smothers her to death. Bigger Thomas murders out of fear and desperation, rather than lust.

Richard Wright is by no means alone among black writers who have presented, through irony, the absurd and often tragic consequences of the savage mode of thinking and racial misconception. In *Invisible Man*, Ralph Ellison's novel, the protagonist is invited to the apartment of a white woman named Sybil, who requests he reveal his savage nature by raping her. "Come on, beat me, daddy — you — you big black bruiser," she moans. She wants her "domesticated rapist" to look at her as if he wants to tear her apart. Outplaying her at her own game, Ellison's hero plies her with drinks ("I rapes real good when I'm drunk") until she passes out. When she awakens he enjoys telling the woman he has not touched, "You brought out the beast in me. I overpowered you. But what could I do?"

In *The Old Glory* (1964) Robert Lowell presents a verse dramatization of Melville's *Benito Cereno*. With subtle updating of Melville's problematical novella to fit contemporary racial conflict, Lowell's play hints at the racial naiveté of white Americans. The white crew of the slave ship is amazed by the revolt staged by slaves they had considered docile and even happy. But once the blacks begin their struggle for freedom, the white crew of the slaver changes its opinion of them. Black people are from that point on considered raging savages to be feared and subdued. The simple-minded and racist Yankee Captain, Amasa Delano, and his equally naive bosun, Perkins, seem to represent a dangerous ignorance and lack of transcending human regard among white Americans. Although Lowell strengthens the tale dramatically by eliminating Melville's tedious court narrative, he also perpetuates the racially ambiguous point of view of Melville's work.

Various literary expressions of black people as savages have been examined in this chapter. Obviously, the range of story, style, and setting within the savage mode is extremely diverse. But there are certain characteristics that link nearly all portraits of the savage. John Saffin's colonial poem, "The Negro's Character" (1701), reprinted in Chatper 1, establishes the central features of the savage mode: "He that exasperates them; soon espies/ Mischief and Murder in thier eyes./ Libidinous and Deceitful, False and Rude,/ The spume issue of ingratitude." Writing influenced by the savage mode almost always comes to a point of revelation or discovery of the "true nature" of black people. The point of view is always that of a white audience, and the discovery is a frightening one. The white figures in these stories invariably discover either "mischief" or "murder." They are confronted with either sexual assault or physical attack. The landscape for these direct or veiled tales of terror is repeatedly a "hideous wilderness," whether actual or psychological. The process of the savage tale is the stripping away of illusion, role, and costume until the essential black man is revealed. This (often literally) naked visage is invariably a frightening one. Often the black figure is vanquished or contained and the reader presumably rests easily. But frequently the intent is fright, the mood is Gothic, and the concluding emotional state is one of terror. *The Emperor Jones* adds a comic dimension to the savage. Brutus Jones is both ridiculed *and* defeated, but the real savage terror, which is the play's chief dramatic effect, remains as a lingering nightmare long after the final curtain.

There seem to be at least two psychological impulses connected with savagism: a compulsion toward the threatening "blackness," as well as flight from the terror evoked. The dominant attitude conveyed in this literature is unmistakable: blacks are an innately savage and frightening race.

3.   The Naturals

> Bruce lay lazy in bed. The brown girl's body was like the
> thick waving leaf of a young banana plant. If you were a
> painter now, you could paint that, maybe. Paint a brown
> nigger girl in a broad leaf waving and send it up
> North.... Get some money to loaf a while longer
> on.... Paint a brown laborer's suave flanks into the
> trunk of a tree. Send it to the Art Institute of Chicago.
> Sherwood Anderson, *Dark Laughter*

Toward the end of the nineteenth century, white Americans
in growing numbers were divorcing themselves from the
farms and small towns of their origins. Ironically, the
further white society moved from its roots, the more it
yearned for and sentimentalized its way of life in earlier
times. As life seemed to move at a faster pace and to take on
complexities previously unknown, large numbers of people
dreamed of escape to a simpler order of things. Most of these
fantasies were satisfied by brief excursions back to nature
and by escapes of the imagination through literature. These
responses can be seen in phenomena such as the "back to
nature" and "rural life" movements of the turn of the
century and in the vogue of the primitive in art and
literature during the 1920s.

In the history of ideas this civilized longing for some
vestige of the primitive is not at all unusual. However, the
effect of continuous simplification of the subjects of
primitivism, who in America have primarily been black,
may severely effect the ability of a dominant society to see
other races and sub-cultures with wholeness and realistic
understanding. Thus a major concern is the kinds of
portraits of black life that white writers have produced when

attracted to the natural mode of primitivism.

Much of the tone and perspective associated with the vogue of the primitive in the 1920s is captured in the epigraph from Sherwood Anderson's *Dark Laughter*. Anderson's protagonist, Bruce Dudley, typifies the search of white Americans of his generation for cultural forms and life styles that seemed more alive than their own. *Dark Laughter* implies that white American society is artistically and sexually anemic. The novel's controlling notion is that the white world, if it is to remain alive must reconnect with the physical elements of life, including sexual fulfillment. (This important strand of the natural mode is developed with particular poignancy by Norman Mailer, who is discussed later). Bruce Dudley represents the search of white culture for the secrets of life renewal, and Anderson felt this revivification could be found best through contact with black culture.

The protagonist leaves his wife, his job, and the boredom of urban life for temporary respite in New Orleans. He watches blacks and learns from them how to relax, to laugh, and to have good sex, an education that eventually transforms his life. But for all that the black women in *Dark Laughter* teach Bruce Dudley, they are silhouette figures. One's impression is chiefly of black faces in windows, black figures in bed, on shipboard, on street corners, and of black laughter. Anderson's New Orleans blacks are stereotyped black "naturals," not whole people; their laughter is never really *dark*.

Irwin Russell's "Christmas Night in the Quarters" (1888) serves well as a brief illustration of cultural primitivism in postbellum Southern literature.[1] Russell's narrative poem contains many of the general characteristics of the natural mode and suggests some of its greatest limitations.

The narrator describes with interest and amusement the antics of the "darkies" at "Uncle Johnny Booker's Ball" on Christmas Eve. But beneath the bromidic observations about happy, simple, fun-loving slaves, Russell comments on the obsession of his *own* people with proprieties, and on the artificiality of their lives:

In this our age of printer's ink
'Tis books that show us how to think—
The rule reversed, and set at naught,
That held that books were born of thought.

The poet sees his white culture as tradition-bound, imitating works and ideas from the past while its own creative talents lie idle. By contrast, he sees among the black people of the slave quarters lives filled with mirth, gladness, and unrestrained expression of feelings because they are "unlearned and untaught" and unfamiliar with the "pedant's rules."

Irwin Russell happens to illustrate many of the features of cultural primitivism even though he takes these ideas only half-seriously. Russell's narrator proffers the opinion that his culture has become artificial and decadent. The models for a simpler, more honest and expressive life are found not so much in the past as in the lives of black people. "Christmas Night" also makes visible the chief limitations of the "natural" mode. In addition to its stereotypes and simplification, this kind of writing shows less interest in black people than in "black life" as symbolic of contrasting values and life styles. Although it may be admirable in providing a corrective or tonic for white civilization, cultural primitivism runs the risk of failing to animate its subjects. If their authors deny them rich and vivid fictional lives, these people once again become slaves to white culture.

Russell and Anderson are but instances of a full gallery of works in which blacks are portrayed as naturals. Considerably fuller and more complex is e.e. cummings's portrait of Jean Le Nègre in *The Enormous Room* (1922). This work is cummings's autobiographical account of his imprisonment by the French government during the First World War. He describes in excruciating detail the indignities and cruelties suffered by his fellow prisoners at La Ferté Macé, a detention center for "security risks" to the French government. cummings and his companion "B" (William Slater Brown) were detained here because Brown had made remarks uncomplimentary to the French in several letters home, and both refused to swear that they "detested all Germans."

But cummings's imprisonment is a gift in disguise. He slowly discovers that he is on a pilgrimage from the diabolical presence of governments at war to the "delectable mountains" of human treasures. In the chapter titled "A Pilgrim's Progress" cummings realizes the transvaluation of his values that is taking place. His newfound "delectable mountains" are a heaven-on-earth of human riches. Among the many new frinds he makes in the enormous jail cell, four individuals stand out. One of the four, a black named Jean Le Nègre, is the man cummings reveres highest among these human treasures: "Of all the fine people in La Ferté, Monsieur Jean...swaggers in my memory as the finest."[2] Although the guards and many of the prisoners look upon Jean as a savage ("le Nègre," "un geant," "black devil"), cummings and "B" become intimate friends with Jean.

Cummings describes Jean's arrival: "Even as the *plantons* fumbled with the locks I heard the inimitable, unmistakable divine laugh of a negro.... Entered a beautiful pillar of black strutting muscle topped with a tremendous display of the whitest teeth on earth. The muscle bowed politely in our direction, the grin remarked musically; *'Bo'jour, tou'l 'monde'*; then came a cascade of laughter. Its effect on the spectators was instantaneous; they roared and danced with joy" (270). Jean's effect on cummings is remarkably like this initial response of the prisoners. His entire portrait of Jean reads more like a description of a child-god come down from some remote corner of Heaven than of a man. He remarks at one point, "May the gods which made Jean Le Nègre give me grace to tell it as it was." Whether he knows it or not, Jean has the power to cast spells; cummings is hopelessly entranced by and in love with his black companion. Their brief prison friendship is as idyllic an example of the longing for fraternity of white and black as will be found in American writing.

Cummings says of Jean, "His mind was a child's; his use of language was sometimes exalted fibbing, sometimes purely picturesque. He courted above all the sound of words, more or less disdaining their meaning" (271). He made up endless word games, becoming a succession of imaginary characters. And when he laughed, "he laughed all over himself." He was "irrevocably vain" and enormously popular with the women prisoners. As the prisoners made their weekly trek to the baths, cummings recalls, "I remember gazing stupidly at Jean's chocolate-colored nakedness as it strode to the tub, a rippling texture of muscular miracle." On another occasion, after Jean has battled with two prisoners, cummings writes that "blood spattered here and there the wonderful chocolate carpet of his skin, and his whole body glistened with sweat. His shirt was in ribbons over his beautiful muscles." It seems obvious that cummings is in love with Jean's body as well as with his laughter and his mind.

Cummings also gives a strikingly individual and loving tribute to his black companion, as this excerpt attests:

And I think of Jean Le Nègre...you are something to dream over, Jean; summer and winter (birds and darkness) you go walking into my head; you are a sudden and chocolate-coloured thing, in your hands you have a habit of holding six or eight *plantons* (which you are about to throw away) and the flesh of your body is like the flesh of a very deep cigar. Which I am still and always quietly smoking: always and still I am inhaling its very fragrant and remarkable muscles. But I doubt if ever I am quite through with you, if ever I will toss you out of my heart into the sawdust of forgetfulness. Kid, Boy, I'd like to tell you: *la guerre est finie.*

  ...Boy, Kid, Nigger with the strutting muscles — take

me up into your mind once or twice before I die (you
know why: just because the eyes of me and you will be full
of dirt some day). Quickly take me up into the bright child
of your mind, before we both go suddenly all loose and
silly (you know how it will feel). Take me up (carefully; as
if I were a toy) and play carefully with me, once or twice,
before I and you go suddenly all limp and foolish. (293)

Cummings's portrait of Jean expresses, of course, much of
the charm and rich playfulness with language that are
synonymous with his poetic style. Beyond his fascination
with French culture and the curious prison itself, cummings
is intent on demonstrating that human treasures can be
found even, or perhaps especially, in a wartime prison
camp. Since *The Enormous Room* is autobiographical, one
must assume that cummings's portrait of Jean has some
substance in fact. Nonetheless, the other black prisoners
were of little interest to cummings. The human treasure
that he discovers in Jean is a black man who is not a savage,
as his fellow prisoners have typed him, but a natural, an
innocent, with a "bright child of a mind" and "gorgeous
laughter." It is cummings's role to reveal the "true" Jean as a
charmer and entertainer, a black Orpheus rather than a
black devil. Like so many of his counterparts in the
literature of the natural mode, Jean is an innocent, oblivious
to the workings of the penal system and to the war itself.
Even commings's tone is subtlely condescending; he is
amused by the avid if not fawning appreciativeness of his
black friend. Cummings is attracted to Jean Le Nègre, one
may speculate, for the usual reasons that whites are attracted
to primitivism in its natural mode. It allows them to indulge
in a primitive outlook and lifestyle they may admire or feel
deprived of, but which they would not wish to permanently
adopt.

Thus, in place of a full portrait, cummings leans heavily
on some of the traits that are stock-in-trade with the natural
mode: childlike simplicity and naiveté, a pastoral or rustic

life, music, laughter, and a seemingly harmonious, natural integration of occupation and life style. Cummings's portrait also points to the tendency in more recent white literature to replace the savage with the natural as the "true" nature of black character.

WILLIAM FAULKNER

William Faulkner has written at length in his novels about civil rights and race relationships in the South. His novels contain a great many images of black life and some half-dozen significant black portraits. Because of the range and number of Faulkner's black portraits and his several critical studies depicting black life, the discussion here is confined specifically to his black naturals in *Sartoris, The Sound and The Fury,* and *Go Down, Moses.*[3] Equally important, although not within the focus of this book, is Faulkner's exploration of the character and circumstance of the "tragic mulatto" through his portraits of Charles Bon in *Absalom, Absalom!,* Joe Christmas in *Light in August,* and Lucas Beauchamp in *Intruder in the Dust.*

Fundamental to Faulkner's ideology is a powerful love of nature and rustic simplicity. This love forms a vital and dynamic presence in his fiction and shapes the values he regards most highly. Many of Faulkner's characters are at home in nature; they live by the rhythms of the soil and seasons and are alive to the subtlest details, but none of them, as Cleanth Brooks puts it, "enjoys the kind of mystic communion which the early Wordsworth seemed sometimes to experience...nor do Faulkner's characters often find in nature the Wordsworthian healing of the distraught spirit."[4] Yet, like Wordsworth, Faulkner finds in nature a special power to form and shape human character that does not exist in civilization. Both writers invest special interest and care in children, idiots, and peasants. When asked to express his

feelings about nature and civilization, Faulkner's comments
seem almost to paraphrase Wordsworth's "Lines Written in
Early Spring":

> To her fair works did nature link
> The human soul that through me ran;
> And much it grieved my heart to think
> What man has made of man.

Faulkner puts it this way: "I think that man progresses
mechanically and technically much faster than he does
spiritually, that there may be something he could substitute
for the ruined wilderness, but he hasn't found that."[5]

The importance of nature to Faulkner can also be evidenced
in the fate of his antagonists, all of whom have in some sense
denied nature. The frustration, alienation, and confusion of
Faulkner's civilized figures stem most often precisely from
their separation from nature. As a result of the accumulated
artifice and artificiality of their lives they are unable to
respond naturally and spontaneously to experience.
Faulkner's sympathies are with a much less rational, less
cerebral approach to life. The people he most admires are, as
Brooks has observed, "simple in mind and spirit and have
managed to maintain the kind of wholeness and integrity
that we associate with childlike sincerity and lack of duplicity."[6] He shows a special affection for such earthy figures
as Lena Grove of *Light in August*, Dilsey, Sam Fathers, and V.
K. Suratt, the sewing machine salesman in *Sartoris*. There is
about these figures an unquestioned acceptance of life, yet
also sufficient toughness of character to survive in Faulkner's
world.

Even among his many primitive characters Faulkner's
blacks are set apart. Edmund Volpe believes that for
Faulkner "the Negro is close to his sources in the natural
world. Only a few generations removed from the jungle, his
accumulated social heritage has not yet conditioned his

responses, choked off his natural feelings."[7] Sam Fathers, more than any other of Faulkner's primitives, epitomizes these qualities. Cass Edmonds tells his young cousin, Ike, that the blood of Sam "knew things that had been tamed out of our blood so long ago that we have not only forgotten them, we have to live together in herds to protect ourselves from our own sources."[8] Edmonds's comment, in context, is a good illustration of cultural primitivism. It is based on the belief that nature is good and man, in nature, is a noble creature. Faulkner relates that "there was something running through Sam Father's veins which runs through the buck too." By watching, listening to, and emulating a man like Sam Fathers, who is of white, Indian, and black parentage, one could achieve harmony with himself and his environment.

At the heart of all cultural primitivism is the notion that civilized man has much of value to learn from nature and from primitive people; this is the attitude held by Ike McCaslin and Cass Edmonds regarding Sam Fathers, and by Faulkner regarding many of his black characters. In his discussion of Faulkner's black portraits, Irving Howe comments that no other white American novelist "has watched the Negroes so carefully, patiently." As Howe aptly expresses it, Faulkner's racial outlook also changes over the years: "His early assurance melts away, his sympathies visibly enlarge; but always there is a return to one central image, the image of memory and longing."[9] The search for lost fraternity of black and white is at the center of Faulkner's primitivism. Although his portraits in this vein are handled with greater skill and complexity later in his career, the basic function of the "primitive" figure is established in *Sartoris* (1929), is further developed in *The Sound and the Fury* (1929), and receives its fullest treatment in *Go Down, Moses* (1940). These three works will trace the range and function of Faulkner's blacks as cultural primitives. In each of the three his blacks stand in contrast to a society weakened by loss of traditional values. In *Sartoris*, black "naturals" save or attempt to save whites from their cultural ills. In *The Sound and the Fury*, Dilsey Gibson, the Compsons' black mammy, is Faulkner's exemplar of integrity, strength of character, and the preservation of moral values. "The Bear" is Faulkner's fullest expression of primitivism in the natural mode, dramatizing its sometimes didactic function through Sam Father's instruction of Ike McCaslin.

In Faulkner's early novels, notably *Soldier's Pay*, *The Unvanquished*, and *Sartoris*, one finds many thin, facile, and grossly stereotyped images of blacks. Racial slurs and derisively comic figures are numerous. *Sartoris* serves abundantly as an illustration of the general insensitivity and carelessness to be found in Faulkner's early treatment of blacks.

*   *   *   *   *

Sartoris (1929) focuses on the struggle of young Bayard Sartoris, a soldier just returned from the First World War, to come to terms with himself and his family. Toward the end of the novel Bayard visits the MacCallums, a white family living on the verge of Yoknapatawpha's wilderness country. After several days of hunting and easy drinking, Bayard leaves the MacCallums and turns his pony toward the lonely, silent woods. This is the most detailed picture one has, in *Sartoris*, of the primitive landscape. "The hills rose wild and black about them. No sign of any habitation, no trace of man's hand did they encounter."[10] Finally Bayard comes upon a cabin, awakens the black couple living there, and asks for shelter and food. He and his horse are given shelter in the black man's barn. The next day — Christmas morning — the couple share their meager meal, and Bayard passes around his jug of whiskey. The scene is handled with great care; it is something of a Christmas communion between the two races, and it would change the direction of the novel if Bayard were not bent on self-destruction.

Those white critics who have commented on the scene have remarked of its beauty, is sensitivity, its fidelity to black life. Cleanth Brooks, for example, observes, "in the scene the Negroes are treated with a scrupulous fidelity to the facts of the situation, and it is they who come off well in the scene, not the deracinated Bayard."[11] One cannot quarrel with Brooks or with Irving Howe, who sees in the scene "an interlude of quiet and decorum."[12] In fact, one's concern is with the beauty of this and similar scenes handled in the natural mode. The black family Bayard visits remain nameless, and they refer to him as "white folks." For all that is invested in the scene, it is an empty, symbolic encounter of white and black. Here, as elsewhere in his fiction, when Faulkner brings together blacks and wilderness landscape, they function as a unified counterforce to war, industrialization, and crumbling Southern aristocracy.

Despite its many weaknesses, *Sartoris* is usually viewed as a threshold novel that develops many of the themes appearing in Faulkner's later fiction: "The deterioration from the past, the clash of past and present, the alienation of man from nature,"[13] as Volpe states them. The central story of the novel traces young Bayard's arrival home from the war, his unsuccessful attempts to become a Sartoris and a civilian again, and his eventual death in an experimental plane not even test pilots would fly. Bayard is burdened by the legends and the tales told him of the Old South and of his family in those days. Volpe sees Bayard's torment stemming from "an oppressive feeling of guilt for having betrayed his heritage."[14] This is partly true, for Faulkner contrasts the rather shabby reality of the Sartorises and Benbows with the glories of the southern past. The immediate reason for Bayard's torment, however, is his anguish over the combat fatality of his brother, Johnny. Bayard not only saw Johnny's plane shot down, but he believes he could somehow have saved his brother.

Bayard either lies sleepless at night, in auguish, or drinks himself to a sleep filled with nightmares of his brother's burning plane. During the day he tries to vent his grief and frustration by riding wild horses or ramming through the sleepy countryside in his roadster, with a "roar of sound like blurred thunder." His presence in the otherwise placid landscape is cyclonic — upsetting wagons, shattering the heavy silence. His sports car becomes a civilian equivalent to his fighter plane, plunging through the landscape as if in search of the enemy craft that downed his brother. Throughout *Sartoris* Bayard's car symbolizes the effect of the industrialized twentieth century on traditional values, the older America, and on the south. Against Bayard and the roadster Faulkner juxtaposes the land and its primitive folk.

One of the most telling of these confrontations begins with the unruffled quietude characteristic of simple pastorals: "The road descended in a quiet red curve between pines through which the hot July winds swelled with a long sound like a far-away passing of trains, descended to a mass of lighter green willows, where a creek ran beneath a stone bridge." The only other sounds are "the liquid whistling of a quail somewhere," and "the long sough of the wind among the sober pines" (206). But there has been another sound, for John Henry had his father have stopped their mule-drawn wagon to listen. It might have been a tree falling, the younger man thinks. Then they see the roadster. It seems to take ages before John climbs down to the overturned car, unafraid of it or what white men might say about his meddling — just knowing that a white man must be trapped inside the vehicle, now half-submerged in the stream. Despite his father's pleas ("Don't you tech him. White folks be sayin' we done it," 207), John Henry extricates Bayard and carries him up the bank to their wagon.

The trip to the Sartoris place on John Henry's wagon is pure torture for Bayard; each lurch of the wagon jams his broken ribs into his flesh. John Henry holds his hat in front of Bayard's face to shield him from the savage sun. Bayard's head rests on Henry's knees as the black man holds him, trying to make the trip bearable.

It is a reasonable conjecture that Faulkner chose the name John Henry because of the black folk hero of that name. The legendary John Henry is a "natural man," according to the ballads, who battles and defeats a steam drill that threatens his job and those of other black workers on the "C & O Line." This parallel to Faulkner's character is revealing, since Faulkner frequently juxtaposes black men and machines as if they were naturally opposed forces. As with the legendary description of John Henry, Faulkner's blacks are, with few exceptions, versions of the "natural man." But there are some important differences. The John Henry of ballad and legend is acutely aware of the threat of industrialization to his way of life. Not only is he cognizant of the forces at work about him, but he attempts to alter them by competing with the steam drill — a contest that takes his life, even though he beats the machine. He is a folk hero rather than a "natural man."

The contrasing function of Faulkner's John Henry is quickly apparent. Like the nameless black family that shelters Bayard on Christmas Eve, he is a symbol of the natural man, of an older way of life that is close to the soil, simple, dignified, productive, and enduring. He stands as counterpoint to those forces of the twentieth century Faulkner so violently dislikes: the effects of the war, the machines of violence, the disintegration of traditional values. Faulkner's John Henry has no discernible understanding of the forces of change about him. He pulls Bayard from the wreck, holds him on the wagon and shields him from the sun.[16] Bayard is only semiconscious and has practically forgotten the episode by the time he reaches home. The scene sets a pattern followed elsewhere in the novel, and it has no lasting effect upon any of its participants.

Bayard's second auto mishap causes his grandfather's

death and is a turning point in the novel. Unable to face the rest of his family, Bayard has one of the servants take in the body and bring around his horse. Riding toward the hill country, he spends the next few days with his friends the MacCallums. There is about the MacCallum clan a continual sense of order, decorum, tranquility, and family affection. They have a rhythm of life that does not stop short to embrace Bayard; he either becomes a part of it — the breakfasts at dawn, the 'possum and fox hunts, the quiet talk around the blazing fire — or not. For a time Bayard seems to become at one with this way of life.

Faulkner's handling of this "primitive" white family is most revealing. The pace is leisurely, the writing detailed and controlled. Irving Howe calls it "the only first rate section of *Sartoris*."[17] The portraits of old Virginius MacCallum and his sons, Rafe and Buddy, are richly and colorfully drawn. Faulkner fleshes out the codes, the ideology, the interpretation of history and the civil war by which this family lives. It is this complexity of detail and development that is so conspicuously absent when Faulkner handles the black portraits among his primitive people. They are too often dehumanized to nameless, symbolic figures acting out a farm or woods drama for the benefit of his white protagonists. They are faces, stylized figures, half-invisible people caught up in ritual actions that are not central to their lives. An illustration of this point is the scene that began this discussion of *Sartoris*.

Bayard has worn out his welcome at the MacCallums by the day before Christmas. They do not know of his grandfather's death and assume that he will certainly return to his family for Christmas Eve. Thus Bayard starts out, although unable to return home. "He turned his pony's head away from town," and on, into the lonely, silent woods. Bayard rides through this wild, dark hill country upon which no man's hand is evident, until he comes to the scant clearing and cabin of the black family. The weather has turned cold; Bayard is lost, frozen, and hungry. The black man leads his horse into the barn and feeds it. Bayard is given a blanket in which to roll himself up. On two occasions he offers the black couple money, but it is ignored. Rather, he must promise he will not smoke if he is to sleep in the barn. "Bayard mounted into darkness and the dry, pungent scent of hay. Here, in the darkness, he made himself a nest of it and crawled into it and rolled himself into the quilt, filth, and odor and all . . ." (343).

With all its parallels to the nativity, there is neither rebirth nor regeneration here. There *is* a ritual sharing of Bayard's jug and of the little food the black family has on hand. There is a communion, jointly offered and consumed, on Christmas Day. Bayard shows a certain warmth toward the black family and a sense of the weight of the day. Given other circumstances the scene could have been meaningful. The black couple share all they have with the white man, including a place in their family on Christmas Day; they help him find his way and they refuse payment. But before many hours pass, Bayard insists that the black man drive him to the railroad, where he pays him exorbitantly. The payment and hasty exit cancel out the spirit of their gifts: Bayard kills himself not long afterward.

Clearly, Faulkner's blacks in *Sartoris* are modeled on the image of the natural man. They are stylized sketches, done in bas-relief. One can, at best, hope Faulkner's racial clichés and general lack of detail in these portraits result from carelessness, rather than from a conscious pejorative. He is much more concerned with contrasting the negative elements of white civilization with the strengths and virtues of black life than with describing that life in detail. Once their function and nature are established, these people are taken for granted or forgotten. Thinly drawn, they can be too easily identified with recognizable figures and situations. John Henry, like the folk hero, is a "natural man" but a good Samaritan as well. Simon, the Sartoris's coachman, clearly resembles the Sambo stereotype (simple-minded, super-stitious, loyal). The black family visited by Bayard seem part of a poorly disguised nativity scene. The field hand, Caspey, is the most sensitively drawn of the black portraits in *Sartoris*, yet even he is something of a "wretched freedman" in his rebelliousness after the war. Once Caspey gets to the woods, however, his desire for social change gives in to his love for nature and hunting 'possum.

Sartoris is both a threshold novel and exemplary of Faulkner's uses of blacks in the natural mode. The function of his blacks is to save, aid, or advise whites in some way, and to stand as silent, almost motionless icons, representing that necessary bondage of man to nature from which most of white society has so disastrously severed itself.

*   *   *   *   *

Although *The Sound and the Fury* (1929) was published the same year as *Sartoris*, it soars light-years beyond *Sartoris* in every respect, including its handling of black portraits. Faulkner's principal black figure here is Dilsey Gibson, mother of three children, who has been a faithful servant and mammy to the Compson family for thirty years. Like John Henry in *Sartoris*, she serves and assists white people, but there is depth and dimension to her character far beyond her counterparts in *Sartoris*. Faulkner shows here a growing interest in black life as a counterforce to the decadence of his major white families in Jefferson.

Dilsey is, as Irving Howe writes, an example of "how a gifted artist can salvage significant images of life from the most familiar notions."[18] Dilsey is a character out of the tradition of the "faithful retainer" and black mammy, but on first reading she does not seem contained and stultified by these stereotypes. She is striking in her ceaseless activity and her attempt to manage the affairs of the Compson household. More than just an efficient servant with a minor role, Dilsey dominates the last of the novel's four sections. She has served the Compsons for three decades and has witnessed their decline in prominence and character. She has taken over responsibility for the spiritual, and many of the physical needs of the family. This has been done not out of ambition but from necessity, since Caroline Compson has abdicated her responsibility for the life of her family. Surrounded by Compsons, Dilsey outlasts "weakness and tribulation," as Faulkner expresses it; she is one "who peacefully shall endure."

In his comments on Dilsey, Faulkner sets the general tone that critics have followed. He refers to the Compsons as a tragic family, a family set apart from "Dilsey, the Negro woman, she was a good human being. That she held that family together for not the hope of reward but just because it was the decent and proper thing to do."[19] Generally speaking, Faulkner's critics have incorporated his comments into their assessment of Dilsey, seeing her as a symbol of moral virtue and courage, and as foremost among all the Faulkner characters who have the strength to endure.

The issue to resolve is whether Faulkner sufficiently dispenses with the traditional stereotype of the mammy and the shallow function of blacks in his early novels. Is Dilsey sufficiently realized as a private and public self to be convincing in her role as a center of meaning and value in the novel? Not only must she serve the doomed Compson family, but she must serve as Faulkner's counterforce, as an exemplary life that will outlive the Compsons as it outshines them.

"The day dawned bleak and chill on Easter Sunday, April 8, 1928,"[20] Faulkner writes. In the grey morning light Dilsey emerges from her cabin, "a stiff black straw hat perched atop her turban," and wearing a "maroon cape with a border of mangy and anonymous fur above a dress of purple silk"

(281). Faulkner pauses to set the day and to set Dilsey's character and dress, to describe how her clothing draped over her bony frame, across her fallen breasts, and then ballooned about her hips, above her many petticoats. Once a big woman, she is now, except for a paunch and the sagging skin, more a skeleton on which both muscle and tissue are tautly stretched. This is not a flattering portrait, of course, but neither is it condescending.

Throughout the novel Dilsey is in action, in motion, preparing meals and cleaning up, tending to the needs of Benjy and the other Compson children, and interceding in the endless arguments between the family members. Dilsey seldom argues the substance of the debates but rather seeks simple solutions and desires peace, harmony, and quiet throughout the household. Much of her energy is expended trying to wrest peace and quiet from the endlessly battling Compsons. Her voice rings through the kitchen, pleading, "Hush now," "Hush, Miss Cahline," "Hush now, Jason," "Hush yo mouf, Luster."

As to her kitchen, she runs it like a superannuated, overstrained general. On this particular April morning Luster has overslept and there is no fire in the woodstove. Dilsey is obliged to haul her own stove wood, light the fire, heat water for Caroline's hot water bottle, prepare breakfast for the family, get Benjy dressed — and all this in silence so Jason can continue sleeping. Dilsey has learned over the years to deal with Caroline Compson with firmness and patience: "you put hit down and g'wan back to bed," Dilsey tells Caroline, who is holding the hot water bottle. She deals with all domestic matters with similar resolve. There is very little that is servile or submissive about Dilsey, and it is these qualities, along with patient persistence through three decades of Compson adversity that have won her so many admirers.

As the burdensome Easter morning progresses, it is discovered that Quentin, Caddy's daughter, has stolen

Jason's secret hoard from his strong box and run away. Jason is furious and will soon race off toward Mottstown in pursuit. Once the chaotic breakfast is completed, Dilsey heads for church with Ben, Frony, and Luster. Frony objects to bringing Benjy to their church, because there are "folks talkin." The opinion among certain of Jefferson's whites is that even "a white idiot" is too good for a black church. This provides Dilsey with another occasion to display fidelity to her principles. She replies, "Den you send um to me. Tell um de good Lawd don't keer whether he smart er not. Dont nobody but white trash keer dat" (306). Naturally, this is said in confidence to her daughter rather than to a white person, but it does display the strength of Dilsey's convictions and the sharp independence of her tongue.

At church, several young black children recoil at the sight of Benjy. Yet how differently Faulkner treats this scene than Stephen Crane handled a similar scene in "The Monster." Here Faulkner never loses sight of Ben's essential humanity:

"I bet you wont go up en tech him."
"How come I wont?"
"I bet you wont. I bet you skeered to."
"He wont hurt folks. He des a loony."
"Dat un wont. I teched him."
"I bet you wont now."
"Case Miss Dilsey lookin." (307)

Evident once again is the evenness of Dilsey's love for the Compson children, her protectiveness of Ben, and her determination to make life as meaningful for him as she can.

The Easter service builds around the sermon delivered by Reverend Shegog, a visiting St. Louis preacher, and deliver it he does! This brief sermon is the basis for one of Faulkner's greatest scenes. It also shows some of his boldness in giving lifelike individuality to his minor black characters, in contrast to the shallow black figures that people his early novels. Reverend Shegog is described as having the face and

wizened body of a monkey. Is this caricature or pejoration?
The answer seems clear after hearing the last lines of his
sermon:

"I sees de resurrection en de light; sees de meek Jesus
sayin Dey kilt Me dat ye shall live again; I died dat dem
whut sees en believes shall never die. Breddren, O
breddren! I sees de doom crack en hears de golden horns
shoutin down de glory, en de arisen dead whut got de
blood en de ricklickshun of de lamb!"

By the end of the sermon Dilsey is deeply moved, rigidly
and quietly crying. The sermon has provided her with
spiritual insight and renewal. Not only does the sermon give
strength to her life through the power of its rhetoric and the
vividness of its Easter imagery, but it helps her to see and
pass judgement upon the Compson family. Dilsey leaves the
church, tears streaming down her face, and says to Frony,
"I've seed de first en de last. Never you mind me." Then, a
moment later, she restates the image that, like an epiphany,
has swept across her consciousness: "I seed the beginnin, en
now I sees de endin" (315). The most immediate explanation
of these alpha and omega references could be within the
context of the Christian year, from Christmas to Easter. But
it seems clear that Faulkner intended further application of
the Easter sermon and Dilsey's response to it than this.
    Later in the day, as she returns to the chaos of the
Compson household and inquires for news about Quentin
and Jason, Dilsey repeats the words that weigh so heavily
upon her, "I seed de first en de last" (316). It is clear now that
the tears were also for the Compsons, who seem doomed to
self-destruction despite all Dilsey's efforts to the contrary.
She weeps for Benjy as a mother for her wounded child.
Dilsey's tears are presumably Faulkner's tears, too, as more
than one critic has suggested, tears for the old order in its
passing, and for the failure of Faulkner's generation of

southerners to find sufficient strength and moral courage to do more than survive.

The wide range of critical interpretations of Dilsey's role in the novel is itself evidence of the heavy ideological burden Faulkner places on the black woman's shoulders. Lawrence Thompson focuses on Dilsey as one of the four centers of consciousness in the novel.[21] In his interpretation, the Dilsey section and the Benjy section that opens the novel form a frame of love and human regard that contrasts with the self-destructiveness and greed of the Quentin and Jason sections. Parts I and IV provide order through self-sacrifice and compassion, an order that does not balance but at least stands against the narcissism and excessive idealism of Quentin, the cruelty and hatred of Jason.

Dilsey has also been seen as an expression of the archetypal feminine. David Williams argues that Dilsey is the only maternal figure in the novel, having raised all the white and black children in the two families. Williams also sees her, in archetypal terms, as the "mother of the dying god." On Easter morning she sees, for the first time in her life and in a moment of unitary vision, that the experience of the feminine encompasses both birth and death. As Williams puts it, "Faulkner brings an incarnation of a pagan diety, the great mother, into the present world. She is formed in all her significance by the symbols of authentic primtivism."[22]

The wide range of symbolic and even archetypal interpretations of Dilsey reinforces what is already clear: Faulkner uses Dilsey as a life-force to stand against the destructiveness of the Compsons and all they represent in his fictional portrayal of the human condition. What Faulkner does with Dilsey's character, as a center of meaning and strength, is both praiseworthy and unsettling. He is working within a long tradition of cultural primitivism in which whites have seen blacks as admirable for their simple virtues, their natural strength and integrity, their ability to persevere and endure despite adversity. The general defect in portraits of this sort is that they greatly simplify the life of the so-called primitive. When the formula of the black natural is applied, it is generally at the expense of individual character. Black naturals are depicted as physically, sexually, musically, maternally, or spiritually superior, but seldom are they allowed to express ambivalence and uncertainty, to show weakness and error, or to possess the idiosyncrasies of individual behavior that will make them lifelike as well as symbolic. To return to the question posed earlier in this section: does Faulkner sufficiently vivify Dilsey with enough character life to support the burden of her meaning?

This is as irreverent a question to ask as it is difficult to answer. Dilsey is much loved by Faulkner and probably by most of his readers. However, the very sentiment so easily attached to one's affection for Dilsey may be a clue to certain weaknesses in Faulkner's handling of her character. For all that he invests in Dilsey, he nevertheless treats her with sentimentality and paternalism. Irving Howe rather delicately expresses this viewpoint: "The conception behind Dilsey does not seriously clash with the view of the Negro that could be held by a white man vaguely committed to a benevolent racial superiority."[23] Faulkner's dedication of *Go Down, Moses* to his own mammy gives a clear image of this sentimental recollection.

> To Mammy
> CAROLINE BARR
> Mississippi
> (1840-1940)
> Who was born in slavery and who
> gave to my family a fidelity without
> stint or calculation of recompense
> and to my childhood an immeasurable
> devotion and love.

It seems likely that much of Faulkner's loving regard for Caroline Barr animates his portrait of Dilsey Gibson. He had perhaps too many rich memories to create a mammy figure who revealed a life beyond her role as a figure of strength, fidelity, "devotion and love."

It is surprising how little is known about Dilsey as a black woman, given the vividness of her portrait. She has a husband named Roskus, who also works for the Compsons, three children — Frony, T. P., and Versh — and a grandson named Luster. Strangely enough, for all the love and affection Dilsey lavishes on the Compson children, she is usually harsh and threatening to her own. Not once in the novel is there a show of warmth or affection for her own family. Faulkner establishes the fact that Dilsey lives in two worlds — he describes the black church service in fine detail — but he does not show Dilsey as a mother to her own family and as a woman in the black community, except very briefly in the Easter morning scene. In fact, closer inspection of her presence in the novel reveals that her speech and gestures are surprisingly repetitious. Her characteristic expression is "hush"; her endless effort is to pacify, to silence, to bring peace and love to the Compsons. Perhaps because she cannot be candid in her response to the Compson children, she responds more harshly to her own. The image of Dilsey in motion that Faulkner prints so indelibly upon his readers' imaginations is of the black woman climbing the Compson's stairs. Again and again the reader sees her "dragging her feet and grunting and groaning like they were straight up and three feet apart." (273-74). Faulkner gives detailed insight into the psychic landscape of all his other major characters; where is the stream-of-consciousness monologue that would reveal the rich complexity and ambivalence that must reside within Dilsey as well? Surely, after presenting Benjy's interior monologue Faulkner could have hurdled the racial barrier to give Dilsey the fullness her role demands. Instead, there is a series of stereotyped gestures prefunctorily repeated, the one exception being the Easter morning church scene. Faulkner allowed Dilsey to keep her dignity, but in doing so denied her a mind and consciousness separate from her role in the Compson family.

Faulkner probably fails to give Dilsey a mind and to record her thoughts because such a portrait would have revealed too much. True to the tradition of the natural, Faulkner must have felt it necessary to keep Dilsey innocent of history and of racial consciousness. Perhaps he did not wish to see her as mother to her own children, for doing so would render her too lifelike for the sentimentalized and symbolic character he conceived. As Faulkner himself expresses it, "In the whole family there was Dilsey that held the whole thing together and would continue to hold the whole thing together for no reward, that the will of man to prevail will even take the nether channel of the black man, black race, before it will relinquish, succumb, be defeated."24 What is fascinating here is Faulkner's movement, practically in the same breath, from Dilsey as a character to Dilsey as a symbol of man's struggle to endure and prevail. His racial slur stands as if to compensate for his tribute, through Dilsey, to black strength and character.

By contrast to what has preceded her, Dilsey represents considerable growth in Faulkner's presentation of black character, which sees her as a symbol for certain black strengths and virtues missing in white' society. Dilsey and Sam Fathers (in *Go Down, Moses*) are cultural primitives serving as anchors to windward for the white families who depend upon them.

*   *   *   *   *

Faulkner's next sizable portrait of a black natural is of Sam Fathers. The scene shifts from the Compson to the McCaslin family, and from Jefferson to the unaxed wilderness region in the bottomland along the Tallahatchie River. The topic shifts from the death of a white family to the death of the wilderness. Just as Dilsey has been all but biological mother to the Compson children, so Sam is a paternal figure to the fatherless young white boy, Ike McCaslin, whom he initiates into those wilderness virtues that Sam has lived by. Faulkner's portrait of Sam is far more complex than that of Dilsey; it stretches through several stories and reveals his life from first to last. Although Sam's father was a Chickasaw Indian chief, his mother was a quadroon slave, and thus the blood of the three races flows through his veins. Sam has been forced to live the life of a black man, first as a slave and then as a faithful servant to the McCaslins. Thus, despite his Indian heritage, Sam must be considered a black man, for this is the life he has had to live. Of central issue here is whether Faulkner manages to give Sam Fathers the fullness and life-giving richness of character he omitted in his presentation of Dilsey.

*   *   *   *   *

Go Down, Moses (1940) and its celebrated story "The Bear" include Faulkner's fullest, most revealing portrait of a black natural. Like so many of Faulkner's characters, Sam Fathers appears in a number of works: *Intruder in the Dust, The Reivers,* and the stories "Red Leaves," "The Old People," "A Justice," "The Bear," and "Delta Autumn." Through these stories Faulkner seems to present a character dilemma: Sam has lived a life of complex circumstances; his teachings suggest a wide understanding of the natural world and of human conduct, yet he reveals little awareness or under-standing of the forces that have affected his life.

In Faulkner's story "The Old People" one learns that Sam's father, Doom, is a nephew to the old chief, Ikkemotubbe. When Doom returns from his adventure in New Orleans be brings with him a French companion, the

Chevalier Soeur-Blonde de Vitry, and a quantity of arsenic contained in a "gold snuff box." To display his new power gained from the white men, he "took one of the puppies from the hamper and put a pinch of white powder on its tongue and the puppy died before the one holding it could cast it away."[25] The next afternoon the young son of Chief Moketubbe mysteriously dies. Moketubbe abdicates that afternoon and Doom becomes "The Man." Shortly after his accession to power, he introduces slavery to the tribe and then a succession of luxuries and artifacts of white civilization, setting in motion the slow deterioration of the Chickasaws and their gradual alienation from the wilderness.

On the day after his accession, Doom conducts a marriage ceremony between the "pregnant quadroon" who had arrived with him and "one of the slave men which he had just inherited (that was how Sam Fathers got his name, which in Chickasaw had been Had-Two-Fathers)" and two years later sells the man and woman and the child, who is his own son, to his white neighbor Carothers McCaslin (166).

By all logic one would expect Sam Fathers, when he is old enough to comprehend it, to reject this corrupt birthright and heritage from Doom, but such is not the case. Even though Sam Fathers has been a slave much of his life, "his face and bearing were still those of the Chickasaw chief" (164). Ike's older cousin, Cass, tells Ike that Sam " 'probably never held it against old Doom for selling him and his mother into slavery" ' and that Sam " 'probably believed it is the chief's blood which was 'betrayed' through the black blood which his mother gave him' " (168). Most likely Cass's interpretation is correct. Sam shows little interest in his fellow blacks on the McCaslin plantation, having always considered himself above them as the son of an Indian chief.

With the death of Jobaker, the last full-blooded Chickasaw, Sam must feel that the heritage of the wilderness is at last his, despite the mixture of the three bloods in his veins. The morning after burying Jobaker, Sam demands of Cass

Edmonds that he be released to live in the woods in order to take Jobaker's place there. " 'I want to go," ' he said, " 'Let me go.' " And then " 'I'm going now' " (173), not even waiting for Cass to react. Sam not only replaces Jobaker as high priest and chief of the Chickasaw wilderness, but he also sets himself free. As Cass tells Ike, " 'He was born in a cage and has been in it all his life; he knows nothing else' " (167). Life as a black man has been lifelong imprisonment for Sam.

Now, at last, he can be an Indian, the last chief of the Chickasaws. What Sam does not admit is that his kingdom, the great woods, is already corrupted and doomed. He is at last reestablished as his father's son, yet it was his father who sold Sam and his mother into slavery. It was also his father who doomed the wilderness — by selling it to white men — and doomed the Chickasaws by introducing slavery and "civilizing" his people. The patrimony Sam now assumes for a brief tenure is almost as corrupt as the patrimony Ike inherits and rejects in part IV of "The Bear." There is, of course, no way of knowing whether he decides to claim the tainted patrimony regardless. One knows only that Sam chooses freedom (" 'Let me go,' " " 'I'm going now' "), the great woods, and his Indian heritage over the race and heritage of his mother. Ironically, it was his mother's line that was more nearly uncorrupted, that had retained its strength and its ability to endure, despite — or perhaps because of — its subjugation.

Even if Sam Fathers, in his old age, has idolized his Chickasaw heritage to the exclusion of his black heritage, his function in "The Bear" is heightened by his "dual" fatherhood. Although he becomes a spiritual father to a fatherless Ike McCaslin, one should remember that his name has been shortened from the original, "Had-Two-Fathers." Cass explains to Ike that Sam is " 'himself his own battleground, the scene of his own vanquishment and the mausoleum of his own defeat' " (168). His black blood has been vanquished and enslaved by the blood of his white and Indian ancestors. In leaving the plantation for the wilderness, Sam imagines that he has set himself free from the warfare within him and from the conflict between civilization and wilderness that has always surrounded him. He believes that he is living, at last, the role for which he was born, forgetting or ignoring the corruption that role represents.

Thus the saga presented in "The Old People" and in parts I-III of "The Bear" is an idyll, a romance of the most incantatory nature. It resides outside of time, as a hiatus during which the slow but ceaseless hacking of civilization against the fact and the spirit of the wilderness seems temporarily suspended. William Van O'Connor has described the tone of "The Bear" as almost hallucinatory in its power to convince the reader of the existence of a world of no sin, no evil, no injustice. It is as if Faulkner wishes to stop time and the flux of history before the close of his frontier and the death of the living spirit of his wilderness. Along with Faulkner the reader can savor once more this land and its people, pure and intact. For a time civilization and racial injustice and the bankers of Jefferson and the logging concerns from Memphis must wait while one observes the dimension and power of this land as it might have been before settlement. On this aspect of "The Bear" O'Connor comments that "it is a kind of neurotic dream — an escape from, rather than attempt to solve the present injustice."[26] The approaching deaths of Ben, Lion, and Sam are rude reminders that the idyll is drawing forever to a close.

White writers in America have long sought to capture and dramatize scenes of the white man's union with the wilderness he has so greatly devastated and with the non-white, whether with the Indian, whom he disenfranchised and often killed, or with the black man, whom he imported and enslaved. Cooper describes this romance of regained innocence and lost love in the relationship of Natty Bumpo and the Indian chieftain, Chingachgook. In his *A Week on the Concord and Merrimack Rivers* Thoreau creates a similar romance in the friendship of the white fur trader Alexander Henry and the Indian Wawatam. Mark Twain alters the theme, making the white boy's fraternal companion a runaway slave rather than an Indian. By contrast to the decadence and deceit along the Mississippi's shores, the river itself, much like Faulkner's Yoknapatawpha wilderness, presents a detached setting in which this otherwise impossible friendship of Huck and Jim can occur.

Throughout his fiction Faulkner shows a tenderness for the dream of childhood friendships between blacks and whites, especially in *The Unvanquished, The Sound and the Fury,* and the short story "The Fire and the Hearth." Melvin Backman comments that "in *Go Down, Moses* the love that has been destroyed is the brotherhood between black and white."[27] In the relationship of Sam and Ike, Faulkner brings together two powerful themes: this much-longed-for brotherhood of white and non-white (Sam is of black, white, and Indian blood) and, through Sam, the equally longed-for reunion of the white man with the primordial wilderness. However, this is not the mere friendship of two youngsters that Twain's portrait of Huck and Jim too often resembles. It is the kinship of a young, parentless white boy with a black man old enough to be his grandfather and who teaches him the wisdom he has learned from the wilderness.

Sam is waiting at the threshold of the wilderness on the day of Ike's first trip to the Big Bottom. Faulkner captures that unforgettable sense of the big woods — "great, brooding, seemingly limitless" — as Ike approaches it for the first time. The woods seem like a great wall, "tremendous and still and seemingly impenetrable in the gray and fading light." At this moment Ike begins "his novitiate to the true wilderness." He sits in the wagon with Sam, "the two of them wrapped in the damp, warm negro-rank quilt while the wilderness closed behind his entrance as it had opened momentarily to accept him" (195). From this November hunt until Sam's last, nine years later, he indoctrinates Ike in the ways and rituals of hunting and woodsmanship. During the school year Cass instructs Ike in the conventions and procedures of plantation life, but during vacations Sam "teaches him the code of the natural world and leads him back to his source in nature," as Volpe expresses it.[28]

Sam was always a man out of his element on the plantation and acted as if he tolerated his existence there only with great patience. When inclined, he "sharpened plow-points and mended tools and even did rough carpentry work when he was not in the woods." Often the shop would be filled with work awaiting his attention and Sam would be sitting there doing nothing. Yet neither Cass nor his uncles Buck and Buddy before him "ever told him to do or not to do anything that he ever paid any attention to" (168). Sam's integrity to himself and his heritage is unflinching and unaltered by civilization. He is not civilized, not even Christianized by a lifetime of the white man's influence. When he leaves McCaslin's for the woods he carries what few material goods he has accumulated: "He owned so little that he could carry it. He walked."

Cass's notion that Sam leaves for the Big Bottom to establish the distance needed to be Ike's tutor makes very little sense. Sam had always been aloof from Ike, from all people. Rather, his removal from the plantation is a return home to his promised land. Faulkner tells his readers, "There was something running through Sam Fathers' veins which runs through the buck, too." Sam's reconciliation with the wilderness is as the son of the wilderness returned home.

The highest moment in the relationship of Sam and Ike occurs as Sam, serving as priest of the wilderness, baptizes him with the "hot smoking blood" of the first buck the boy kills. Ike is twelve then and it is his third hunting trip to the Bottom. He has already learned to shoot rabbits, to take a stand alone; he has become a better marksman than any of the others except Sam. Ike remembers neither the shot nor the shock of the gun butt. But he remembers being cautioned by Sam to approach the slain buck from behind, and slit his throat. Then "Sam stopped and dipped his hands in the hot smoking blood and wiped them back and forth across the boy's face" (164). The ceremony is that of Ike's confirmation into the wilderness. The warm blood of the deer used to sanctify the induction is the blood of the wilderness that has been tamed out of him by civilization. Through this event and several that follow it, Ike gains a code to live by through understanding and acceptance of nature. The code comprises those virtues that "touch the heart — honor and pride and pity and justice and courage and love" (297).

As familiar as Sam Fathers may seem, one knows very little about him. The images of Sam meeting Ike at the edge of the wilderness, of Sam at the boy's elbow instructing him in the hunt, of Sam daubing the warm deer blood about his face are vivid indeed. But one knows practically nothing of his plans for Ike, or of his comprehension of the forces at work about him in the plantation culture. As with all men of few words, it is easy but perhaps dangerous to assume that Sam knows all. This assumption must be questioned. Sam's instruction combines practicality (woodsmanship, marksmanship, gun safety) and ideology (those values that are a logical extension of the activities of the woodsman-hunter). For example, he tells Ike to distinguish between being scared and being afraid. " 'Be scared. You can't help that. But don't be afraid. A bear or a deer has got to be scared of a coward the same as a brave man has got to be' " (207).

The great difficulty in understanding Sam Fathers arises from the need to interpret and extend the few glimpses of his education of Ike. The process is even more frustrating for young McCaslin. He watches Sam intensely, searching often for some hint or clue in that stoic face. In all his years with Sam the face remains blank, unexpressive, until Ike sees "that faint arching of the nostrils on the first morning when the hounds had found Old Ben" (216). Ike searches desperately for meaning in the face and the laconic instructions; he searches for an inheritance from Sam and the woods, for a way of life. Ike senses the bear will be killed some day and that there are forces afoot that will profoundly alter the world he has entered.

So he should have hated and feared Lion. Yet he did not. It seemed to him that there was a fatality in it. It seemed to him that something, he didn't know what, was beginning; had already begun. It was like the last act on a set stage. It was the beginning of the end of something, he didn't know what except that he would not grieve. He would be humble and proud that he had been found worthy to be a part of it too or even just to see it too. (226)

The opening and closing paragraphs of part II begin with the chant, "So he should have hated and feared Lion." He knows the meeting of Lion and Old Ben is inevitable. When both Sam and Ike have clear shots at Ben but neither can fire, Sam tells the boy, " 'Somebody is going to, some day.' " Ike replies, " 'I know it, that's why it must be one of us. So it won't be until the last day. When even he don't want it to last any longer.' " Ike has now thoroughly absorbed the sense of fatality that hovers about Sam. He is scared of what will happen, of what it will mean, but he is trying desperately not to be afraid.

From the time Sam knows Ike cannot shoot Ben his attention turns almost undividedly to Lion. Ike's lessons are completed, it seems, and he is henceforth virtually abandoned by Sam. The old man refuses to live in the hunting camp, building himself a little hut much like Jobaker's, a quarter-mile away from the others. Even as the hunting party fully believes Old Ben has killed a colt belonging to Major de Spain, Sam knows it is Lion. As the others look at tracks, Ike studies Sam's face for some clue. "There was something in Sam's face now. It was neither exultation nor joy nor hope." Later Ike realizes that what he saw was "foreknowledge." At last Sam knows he has the animal fierce enough to hold Old Ben at bay.

By the conclusion of part III, Ben, Lion, and Sam are dead, and Faulkner's romance of the wilderness has come to an abrupt and shocking conclusion. Neither Ike nor Boon is able to adjust to the changes they have helped bring about. Ike has been initiated into a dying cult. It is perhaps an initiation vow too seriously taken, for it ties him to a set of principles that a man could live by in the wilderness of parts I-III but not in the dying wilderness of Part V. Otis B. Wheeler states, "For Issac [Ike] the golden age was the wilderness time when men lived as brothers before they became tainted by the greed for possession."[29]

Everything about Ike's education hints he is to be the Moses who will lead the South from its racial injustice, its usury of the land, its rapacity, and its decadence. He receives the dual inheritance of the plantation through the McCaslins and the wilderness through Sam Fathers. His education comes at a historic time in American history — during the close of the frontier and the rapid shrinking of the wilderness. All aspects of Ike's education suggest he will be "the man," yet many years after writing "The Bear" Faulkner comments that Ike just did not have the strength of character to be a Moses:

> Well there are some people in any time and age that cannot face and cope with the problems. There seem to be three stages: The first says, This is rotten, I'll have no part of it, I will take death first. The second says, This is rotten, I don't like it, I can't do anything about it, but at least I will not participate in it myself, I will go off into a cave or climb a pillar to sit on. The third says, This stinks and I'm going to do something about it. McCaslin is the second. He says, This is bad, and I will withdraw from it. What we need are people who will say, This is bad and I'm going to do something about it, I'm going to change it.[30]

It is difficult to understand why there is no hint of this weakness during Ike's education under Sam Fathers. At that time Ike shows unusual bravery, courage, and steadiness of

character. The inability to face difficulty or challenge that
comes later is not anticipated in the early parts of the story.
The reason for this, as suggested earlier, is the irreconcilability
of Faulkner's idyll of Ike and Sam with the harsh reality of
the later episodes.[31] Faulkner must have wanted both the
romance and the historic saga, even though the first impedes
the logical development of the second.

Perhaps Faulkner sensed the irreconcilability of the two
portions yet was unwilling to remake his character. Were
Sam to tell Ike about the rapacity of the Chickasaws, about
being sold into slavery by his father, about the doomed
wilderness, the miscegenation and incest in Ike's own family,
clearly this would destroy the simplicity and beauty of those
early scenes and the romance Faulkner indulges in. "The
Bear" pays heavily for its romance in this failure to
illuminate and resolve the many inherent conflicts within
the character of Sam Fathers. Because of his function in
"The Bear" and in Faulkner's ideology, Sam is cut off from
time, from a sense of the forces at work about him, and from
a consciousness of the world in which he lives. Had Faulkner
allowed Sam to reveal his awareness of these forces, even in
his characteristically oblique manner, a much more complex
and admirable portrait would have emerged.

Like Dilsey, Sam is a classic expression of black cultural
primitivism. Both are figures of strength and endurance,
and both stand as models of simple virtues and the old
order. They do not question nor even seem to comprehend
the social forces that are causing radical change all about
them. They endure like the strengths and virtues they
represent. Sam, however, dies with Ben and Lion, and does
not have to witness the lumbering off of the wilderness,
though he must have known it was coming. Dilsey's "I seed
the first en de last" could also be said of Sam, who witnesses
the death of the wilderness spirit, and who has also known
the traditional values of the Chickasaws.

What is true of Sam and Dilsey is true, in general, of

characters Faulkner presents in the natural mode. Products of his sentimental romanticism, they function importantly in his ideology but regrettably have little life of their own. Such is not entirely the case with all of Faulkner's black portraits, however. Charles Bon (*Absalom, Absalom!*) and Joe Christmas (*Light in August*) are expressions of another tradition in black characterization, the tragic mulatto. These two figures are cast in the role of victims because they are trapped between the two races. They represent, for Faulkner, the unsolvable problem of miscegenation and the many fears it releases, and both are killed by whites for the threat they represent to a clean and complete segregation of the races.

Lucas Beauchamp (*Intruder in the Dust*) is Faulkner's fullest and most successful black character. Unlike Dilsey and Sam, Lucas is permitted to express his bitterness, arrogance, and pride. He refuses to humble himself and submit to the customs and expectations of the white man. Of course, his pride comes primarily because his grandfather was L.Q.C. McCaslin, one of the patriarchs of Jefferson. To be seen in his entirety Lucas must be followed through several stories, as well as *Intruder in the Dust.* In "The Fire and the Hearth" Lucas is a young man who refuses to be appropriately submissive. He fights as an equal with a distant white cousin whom he suspects of adultery with his wife, Mollie. It is in "The Bear" that one learns he is the illegitimate grandson of L.Q.C. McCaslin and that he bears his grandfather's first name. Lucas shows his defiance of his white heritage by changing the spelling of his name from Lucius to Lucas. He is Faulkner's most successful black portrait because he is not primarily a cultural primitive or a tragic mulatto but a complex and unpredictable character in and for himself.

It is unfortunate that Faulkner's finest black portrait comes so late in his career, and in a relatively minor novel. Nowhere in Faulkner's fiction does he portray a black character who is a center of consciousness. Nowhere in his writing is there a black character who reveals a mind penetrating enough and who is articulate enough to express his or her life from the inside out, or to speak for black people in some larger or comprehensive sense. In *Intruder in the Dust* Faulkner demonstrates the seriousness of his moral concern over race relations in the south, but he does so only through his white spokesman, Gavin Stevens. Lucas is too self-contained and self-assured in his alienation to speak for anyone but Lucas Beauchamp. One's collective sense of Faulkner's concern indicates that he could and should have produced a black character rebellious and verbal enough to anticipate the growing independence and demand for social justice among southern blacks.

EUDORA WELTY

Because Eudora Welty writes out of the same regional landscape as Faulkner, her black naturals bear certain resemblances: they too seem to white people to be happily natural and at home with their occupations and life situations. Welty richly explores the themes of isolation and alienation and recognizes the presence of these themes in the lives of her black, as well as her white characters. She also focuses fully on individual black characters in three of her stories, giving them a centrality and directness rarely allowed by the writers examined thus far. However, she seldom speculates on the thoughts or inner dialogue of her black characters, and seldom distinguishes between their inner lives and white perceptions of them.

In assessing Eudora Welty's short stories, Louise Gossett comments that "Miss Welty illustrates Pascal's aphorism that 'the greater intellect one has, the more originality one finds in man. Ordinary persons find no difference between men.' "[32] If one were to judge Welty's black portraiture by Pascal's standards, however, her high reputation would be greatly tarnished. The problem is that although Welty's nonfiction shows the sympathy and understanding of a southern liberal toward civil rights and racial injustice, the black portraits in her fiction are sadly thin, unconvincing physiognomies. She is content to sketch in these black portraits in hyperbolic fashion, relying heavily on eccentricities. Only in the story "Powerhouse" does she attempt to crack this surface and speculate on the thoughts and speech of blacks when no whites are present.

Black characters figure significantly in five of her short stories: "Keela, the Outcast Indian Maiden," "A Worn Path," "Powerhouse," "Livvie," and "The Burning." In addition, blacks are thematically significant in the novel *Delta Wedding* and in three nonfiction pieces: "Pageant of Birds,"[33] "Ida M'Toy,"[34] and "Where is the Voice Coming From?"[35]

The three stories discussed here portray blacks as either savages or naturals. In each there is an ironic contrast between the primitivism whites assume to characterize blacks, and the somewhat more detailed portraits revealed by Welty. It is ironic that Welty's implicit criticism of her white characters — their failure to observe their black counterparts as whole, individual, and complex personalities — must also be leveled at her, for she allows the simplifying assumptions of primitivism to stand for detailed portraits of living people.

In most of her fiction Welty shows great concern for individuals who are alienated or isolated from the world. Her characters are frequently victimized, thwarted, trapped in some way. She does not glory in this alienation of her characters, of course, but explores the dreams and fantasies of their special worlds, the better to understand and empathize with them. Her black portraits are no exception to this abiding interest in character types. Isolation and struggle for survival figure prominently along with aspects of primitivism in these stories. Eudora Welty's style is so various, her techniques so subtle, that it is impossible to impose on her black portraits any one generalization. In each of the stories, whites regard blacks as primitives, or make of them primitives, yet in two of the stories Welty attempts to assert an essential individuality and humanity in her black protagonists, even though her whites are unable to perceive it. The pressing question is whether she succeeds in establishing these essential qualities sufficiently for her readers to grasp.

"Keela, the Outcast Indian Maiden" is in reality a mentally retarded, middle-aged black man named Little Lee Roy who was abducted by a traveling carnival for use in its sideshow. As this sordid tale is unraveled, one learns that he had been forced to pose as a savage: an Indian woman who uttered wild shrieks, shook an iron bar to terrify those who approached her cage, and ate live chickens (his only source of food). Lee Roy was whipped so brutally that he dared not revolt.

The story is not Lee Roy's however; it is told by Steve, a young man who worked as a crier for the carnival.

> I remember how the drums was goin' and I was yellin,' "Ladies and gents! Do not try to touch Keela, the Outcast Indian Maiden — she will only beat your brains out with her iron rod and eat them alive!" Steve waved his arm gently in the air, and Little Lee Roy drew back and squealed. "Do not go near her, ladies and gents! I'm warning you!" So nobody ever did. Nobody ever came near her. Until the man.[36]

The mindless audiences reveled in watching a "savage" grunt, howl, suck blood, eat raw meat, and perform the other antics they expected of savages. The situation is truly ludicrous: a little clubfooted black man is made to wear a red dress and stockings, have his face painted red, eat live chickens, and masquerade as a savage Indian maiden. Here are the same starved imaginations, seeking the bizarre and grotesque, that the Duke and Dauphin exploited so successfully while teamed up with Huck and Jim.

Steve tells Lee Roy's story to Max, proprietor of the local

juke box haven. Lee Roy giggles as Steve confesses the enormous burden of guilt he has carried since the odious affair.

"It's all me, see," said Steve. "I know that. I was the one was the cause for it goin' on an' on an' not bein' found out — such an awful thing. It was me, what I said out front through the megaphone." (79)

Steve's guilt has so obsessed him that he has been driven to find Lee Roy and do something to ease his conscience. Exactly what he intends to do is unclear.

Throughout the story Steve and Max stand before Lee Roy, but Steve cannot bring himself to admit Lee Roy's presence, always referring to him in the third person as "she" (Keela), "it" (the savage), and finally "he" (speaking to Max in front of Lee Roy). Steve is too preoccupied with his own guilt and shame to recognize the creature before him. Lee Roy is for Steve a symbol of wronged humanity, but Steve cannot confront the man he has wronged.

Thematically, the story of Lee Roy lends itself exquisitely to Welty's ironic handling of the persistence of "savagism" in the white world she observes. Steve describes Lee Roy's capture this way: "They just kind of happened up on it. Like a cyclone happens: it wan't nuthin' it could do. It was just took up" (84). The carnival could get away with the abduction partly because Lee Roy was retarded but also because he was black and it was the South. The point Welty wishes to make, it seems, is that white society creates its savages (from the most unsavagelike materials) to fit its needs. It puts them in cages, rendering them safe to gawk at. A look at the pitiful "wild animals" found in many roadside zoos indicates that Eudora Welty's "Keela," in all its human grotesquerie, is no isolated observation of American life. It is her intent to expose those elements of the "civilized" world that desire to be "frightened" again and again by the hollow roar of the savage. To compound the absurdity, Lee Roy is made to masquerade as an Indian maiden.

Much of the story's power comes from the ironic contrast of Lee Roy's innocence with the barbaric, terrifying role he is forced to play. Welty doubtlessly picks the most innocent of men to emphasize her point. The savages here are the whites who imprison Lee Roy and those who pay money to experience thrill-terror before his cage, knowing full well that the object before them is no savage.

In the real incident on which Welty based her Lee Roy ("One day I was on an assignment at a fair and talked to a man who has building a booth at the fair grounds. He told me the story I used in 'Keela' — about a little Negro man in a carnival who was made to eat live chickens"),[37] the black man was neither crippled nor mentally retarded.

Although Welty may have made Lee Roy retarded in order to render the abduction and captivity more credible, the effect is disastrous. As a result, Steve is never obliged to address Lee Roy — it would be fruitless. It is also an easy way out for the author; she can merely sketch a stylized figure sitting on the steps of his house, with a bird on his knee and chickens about his feet. Faulkner's masterful handling of Benjy, in *The Sound and the Fury*, suggests the rich possibilities for detailing mental retardation. Beyond that, however, there is no need to make Lee Roy retarded, and its effect on the story is considerable. It means, in essence, that he does not need to be reckoned with. He can be disregarded, and the tragic events of his life reduced to pathos. One feels, somehow, that the suffering and the hurt are less because he is incapable of knowing what has happened to him. His comment at the end of the day to his children virtually reduces him to some inanimate state. He says, "Two white mens come heah to de house. Wouldn't come in. But talks to me about de ole times when I used to be wid be circus" (88). At the end one is left with an image virtually drained of humanity. There is neither understanding nor compassion

for him, even from his children. The fashion in which Welty
builds Lee Roy's character is metonymic; she allows features
such as mental retardation, size, and race to stand for the
whole man. This not only makes Lee Roy a lifeless and
unconvincing character, it seriously lessens the thematic
impact of the story.

"A Worn Path" has received a fair amount of critical
attention, most of it presuming that Eudora Welty intended
her protagonist, Aunt Phoenix Jackson, to be "a symbol of
the immortality of the Negro's spirit of endurance," as
Alfred Appel puts it.[38] The name Aunt Phoenix and the
events of the story appear to parallel the legend of the
Phoenix, thereby suggesting new life for the aged black
woman.[39] Neil Isaacs has suggested that Phoenix's ailing
grandson, to whom she brings medicine and a Christmas
gift, may be seen as the infant Christ. His sickness will be
healed through Phoenix's love and the medicine she brings
from the city.[40] One would think that death, rebirth, and
perpetuation are central concerns in "A Worn Path."
However, Welty may well have intended the title ironically,
for the story she tells is filled with hints that neither Phoenix
nor her grandson will long survive — that "A Worn Path" is
not essentially about perpetuation and the joy of new life.
Beyond her quaint charm, Aunt Phoenix seems too much in
the tradition of the many black uncles and aunties admired
by whites for their humble resignation to the conditions of
their lives.

The story is handled almost entirely from the point of
view of Aunt Phoenix. She inhabits a truly "primitive"
landscape, "out by the old Natchez Trace." The old black
woman, her head tied in a red rag of a bandana, sets out on
an early December morning to walk to Natchez for medicine
to ease the burns in her grandson's throat, caused two or
three years earlier by swallowing lye.

The reason for Phoenix's trip is not apparent until nearly
the end of the story. Instead, one follows the delightful old

woman through forest and field, listening as she talks to
herself and to the plants and animals of her domain:

> Out of my way, all you foxes, owls, beetles, jack rabbits,
> coons and wild animals! . . . Keep out from under these
> feet, little bobwhites. . . . Keep the big wild hogs out of
> my path. Don't let none of those come running in my
> direction. I got a long way. (276)

Eudora Welty creates a woman who is supremely at home
in the primitive landscape. Various signs tell her she should
stay at home in the woods, "and nothing will happen to
you." At the center of the story is the white myth of black
contentment in pastoral or primitive settings. John Edward
Hardy's observations on Welty's use here of the nature myth
are most astute. Welty is aware of this myth of blacks as
"naturals." As Hardy has said, she risks letting this form of
primitivism run away with the story, since it is so seductive
and so skillfully developed. The white reader may identify
with the hunter whom Phoenix meets on her way to Natchez.
When he learns she is walking all the way to town, he laughs,
"Now you go on home, Granny!" He gives another laugh,
filling the whole landscape. "I know you old colored people!
Wouldn't miss going to town to see Santa Claus!" (282). The
point, of course, is that she is not "colored people," that she
is not going to see Santa Claus, and that he does not "know"
her. Perhaps Welty intended the hunter to represent many
of her readers-people who, like the hunter, might think they
know how charming it is to live in the country and how
happy the blacks are who live there. But Welty's reinforcement
of the nature myth throughout the story makes this position
all the easier to maintain. Like the white hunter, the reader
may be tempted to view Phoenix, in Hardy's words, "as one
of a race apart, about whom we are obliged to feel no more
than a certain condescending curiosity."[41]
Appel has observed that when Phoenix begins her return,
bearing the medicine, she is a kind of Magus, "bringing gifts

to a little grandson who, waiting alone, all wrapped up in a quilt, recalls the Christ child in a manger."[42] Appel, Isaacs, and Jones discuss the story in terms of Phoenix's strength of character, her love for her grandson, and the endurance of black people that she exemplifies. What must be added is the context in which these virtues are to be seen. Hardy alludes to this when he refers to the story's "scathing indictment" of white civilization (its self-indulgence, its materialism) and in the "soothing medicine" it offers "to heal the hurts of that 'stubborn case,' black mankind."[43]

The medication Phoenix brings is nothing but a soothing, temporary relief for the permanently injured throat of her grandson. One of the nurses even asks if her grandson has died yet. Since the injury took place three years earlier they probably know that special care is needed to cure th boy; the medicine they dispense merely reopens the throat. Is not the absurdity of many black lives in America symbolized in this situation: the permanent injury, the racist condescension and occasional charity offered by white society, the promises of medication and relief (the white lie — itself another kind of lye)?

Black people are able to survive because they live close to the land, according to the white myth of blacks as "naturals." As Phoenix represents aged endurance, her grandson is the future. One's sympathy is drawn to this image of a grandmother and child wrapped in a patchwork quilt, "holding its mouth open like a bird," partly because it reminds one of the madonna and child. It is difficult to cut through the reverence and romance that cloud the story, however, in order to see the babe as a pathetic image of life caught in the stranglehold of white civilization. What has happened to the child's parents, one must ask, that his grandmother must struggle to keep him alive and give him love?

The greatest danger in this story is in imagining that the little grandson will miraculously recover and Aunt Phoenix

will not have to take the worn path to Natchez again. Then
she could die content in the knowledge that her grandson
would grow strong and become a natural man, as comfortable
in this land as she has been during her long lifetime. But
there are disquieting factors that make this romance
unworkable. White society does not seem willing to incur the
cost of special care; the situation may well remain as it is
until Phoenix dies. The irony of her name lies here; there
will be no "little bird" to perpetuate her life. Rather than
seeing Phoenix consumed by fire and her young rising from
the ashes, one sees instead her offspring slowly *dying* of
ashes, lye being made from wood ashes. The myth of the
phoenix becomes a symbol of fatality in Eudora Welty's
story.

What is ultimately so disturbing about "A Worn Path" is
its very innocence and beauty. Although the story enlarges
itself from a primitive idyll to hint at the nature of black and
white life in the South, it does so entirely outside the
consciousness of Phoenix. Phoenix is clever enough to sneak
a nickel from a white hunter and takes pleasure in getting a
white lady to tie her shoe, but the reader has no more idea
what thoughts cross her consciousness while trudging that
worn path than one has of Sam Fathers's thinking about
slavery and his Chickasaw heritage in Faulkner's "The
Bear." The charm, the determination, the endurance, and
the love are about all one sees in Phoenix's character.
Further, if Welty intended Phoenix to be a metaphor for the
predicament of being black in America, then the implications
of the old lady's naiveté and helplessness are even more
disturbing.

In the story "Powerhouse," Welty explores several different
aspects of the primitivism whites attribute to blacks. But
Powerhouse, a black jazz perfomer, rises above the essential
innocence of Lee Roy and the rustic simplicity of Phoenix,
for he understands the nature of the world he lives in and
has learned to cope with that world through art — through

his mental fantasies and musical improvisations. Despite certain limitations, this story is Eudora Welty's most complex, most perceptive handling of black character.

Powerhouse is a rhythm-and-blues musician from the North who has come to play at a white dance hall in Alligator, Mississippi. Welty wrote the story after attending a dance played by Fats Waller and his band.[44] There is nothing geographically or musically primitive about Powerhouse, yet his white audience, too awed to dance, sees him as such, and believes that they feel the beat of the primitive surging through his music. Technically, he is an anachronism — and "urban primitive," for he combines the spontaneity, freedom from inhibition, the "down home" music of black people with the sophistication, style, worldliness, and savoir faire of the city. Without this last quality no black musician would dare tell a white audience what requests he will play and when he will break for intermission the way Powerhouse does.

Welty handles the description of Powerhouse as if it were the collective feeling of the white crowd. They notice his "African feet of the greatest size"; his mouth, when it opens, is "vast and obscene" and "is going every minute: like a monkey's when it looks for something." His head and belly are enormous; his strong fingers are "about the size of bananas" (254). He is to the white audience both "marvelous" and "frightening," as is "so likely" among "people of the darker race," especially when they are on stage. What is disconcerting about this "white" description of Powerhouse is Welty's failure to distinguish between what she sees, as narrator, and the savagism the white audience attributes to him.

He calls his group "Powerhouse and his Tasmanians," and his attraction to the audience is that of the exotic. He seems to be all the nonwhite races combined:

You can't tell what he is. "Nigger man?" — he looks more

Asiatic, monkey, Jewish, Babylonian, Peruvian, fanatic, devil. He has pale gray eyes, heavy lids, maybe horny like a lizard's, but big glowing eyes when they're open. (254)

In the passage from which the above is taken, Welty tries to convey, in a fleeting, impressionistic style, the images of Powerhouse that might race through a white mind. It is an illustration of the inventive power of the white imagination regarding blacks; Powerhouse stands for everything that is non-Anglo-Saxon, non-Caucasian, non-Western.

The power of this story lies in Welty's development of the Powerhouse who lies beneath the musician — that mask which shakes its "vast cheeks" and has a "leer for everybody." She shows the pain and fear, concealed by the mask, that wells up in the "secret face" of Powerhouse. Although his audience is enchanted, Powerhouse is bored; they are a lifeless bunch. His thoughts begin to wander from his music to his personal life. He imagines he has gotten a telegram about his wife Gypsy: " 'Telegram say — here the words: Your wife is dead' " (259). It is signed "Uranus Knockwood." Other members of the band pick up the fantasy, ask questions, and speculate on how or why Gypsy died. Each improvises on the fantasy as they pile up chorus after chorus of "Pagan Love Song" for the pleasure of the white audience.

By the time Powerhouse announces intermission, the fantasy has gotten too large and lifelike to discard. It dominates their conversation in the World Cafe, as they sip beers during the break. Who is Uranus Knockwood and why did he send the telegram?

"Does? I even know who finds her," cries Powerhouse. "That no-good pussyfooted crooning creeper, that creeper that follow around after me, coming up like weeds behind me, following around after me everything I do and messing around on the trail I leave. Bets my number, sings my songs, gets close to my agent like a betsybug;

when I going out he just coming in. I got him now! I got my eye on him." (267-68)

The fantasy invented to kill time and boredom has by now become a serious creation. Uranus has come to represent all the fears, apprehensions, nameless terrors that can plague a man. Gypsy may be Powerhouse's wife, his woman, or a symbol of all he holds precious and that might be threatened by the Uranus Knockwoods of this world. Soon the others in the band are adding their own versions of this ubiquitous villain:

"He takes our wives when we gone!"
"He come in when we goes out!"
"Uh-huh!"
"He goes out when we comes in!"
"Yeahhh!"
"He standing behind the door!"
"You know him!" (269)

As Powerhouse and his band put this nightmare to music, develop it, improvise on it, they do what black people have done for several centuries: express loneliness and despair through music. Appel comments that "Powerhouse . . . conquers the agony of life through a blues oriented toughness of spirit. In essence, 'Powerhouse' *is* a blues — an extended lament expressed in the short story form."[45] Despite her stereotyping, Powerhouse emerges as the most individualized and fully developed of Welty's black characters.

Appel and others have said of Eudora Welty's characters that, like Faulkner's black characters and earthbound folk, "they endured," that they "withstand and even triumph over their isolation and adversity."[46] This easy conclusion does not bear up against the facts of the stories already examined here. Lee Roy does not triumph over his circumstances. If Steve's guilt is to be seen as Lee Roy's victory, it is a victory none can glory in. The irony of Phoenix is the doubt her specific circumstances cast on the triumph of life over death associated with her name. Should her grandson live, there is little likelihood he will triumph. Like Phoenix, Powerhouse is a figure of remarkable strength and endurance. His triumph over the circumstances of his life is achieved through his imagination and artistry, not through his mastery of his physical environment. "Powerhouse" is the mask he wears to hide his weakness and uncertainties, and the image of "power" whites attribute to him. Welty's blacks suffer and they endure, but they do not "triumph over their isolation and adversity."

Little Lee Roy, Aunt Phoenix, and Powerhouse share a common predicament inasmuch as each is victimized by white characters. Each is a very different combination of primitive traits — and that is just Eudora Welty's point, one suspects. Whites create their blacks to fit their own scenarios. In each story the white imge of blackness and the actual life of the black protagonist have little in common — this is the horror, the grotesqueness Welty must wish to impart. She also fashions her blacks as primitives to fit her purposes.

Louise Gossett comments, "that Miss Welty is sensitive to racial injustice is clear from the story 'Keela.' "[47] This is certainly an adequate thematic assessment of all three stories. The point that must be added, however, is that Welty does not develop her racial portraits with sufficient sensitivity or depth. Appel sees this technique of characterization in all her portraits of grotesques. He writes, "Because they have been treated like things, these characters have been reduced to 'thing-hood,' and the grotesque is a protest against their brutalization and abandonment."[48] This appears to be rationalization to justify a failure in sensibility. The figure of Lee Roy may gain a reader's sympathy but he is too drained of humanity to draw one's empathy or compassion. To a somewhat lesser degree, the romance of the natural figure that surrounds Phoenix and the grotesque animalism of Powerhouse stand instead of richness of character. One of

Ralph Ellison's comments on white writing speaks to the dilemma represented by Welty. All too often the black figure, as Ellison puts it, is pictured as "an over-simplified clown, a beast, or an angel. Seldom is he drawn as that sensitively focused process of opposites, of good and evil, of instinct and intellect, of passion and spirituality, which great literary art has projected as the image of man."[49] Ellison's statement speaks directly to the unsuccessful attempts of both Faulkner and Welty to examine, challenge, and replace primitivisms with whole portraits of black people.

NORMAN MAILER

Turning to Norman Mailer's black portraits, one jumps from the rural South of Faulkner and Welty to the contemporary context of urban America. As Sam Fathers was a natural guide to the territory of Faulkner's wilderness country, so Shago Martin and Mailer's blacks, in general, are supremely at home in the urban jungles of America. They are naturals at self-defense, at sex, in courage, and in the "language of Hip." Like Sam Fathers, Mailer's Shago Martin (in *An American Dream*) also serves the symbolic and priestly function of intiating a white male into new strength, knowledge, and into a realm of action that is to be his inheritance. Curiously enough, Mailer's "The White Negro," his most direct essay on black life and black-white relations, came about following a public insult to and reply from William Faulkner on the topics of school segregation and black sexuality. Coming in the wake of the above scrutiny of Faulkner's and Welty's black portraits, Mailer's portrait of Shago Martin should make even clearer how compelling and continuous has been the idea of the black natural, despite differences in time, topic, style, and place.

Mailer is so extensively a cultural primitivist that a discussion of naturals would be incomplete without consideration of his celebrated essay "The White Negro,"[50] his novels *The American Dream* (1964) and *Why Are We in Vietnam?* (1967), his portrait of Mohammad Ali in *The Fight* (1975), and his essays on black power that appeared in *Existential Errands* (1972).

Mailer's *Advertisements for Myself* (1959) declares for all time the great significance he places on his own work. In his preface Mailer states." The sour truth is that I am imprisoned with a perception which will settle for nothing less than making a revolution in the consciousness of our time." This is, of course, characteristic Mailer bravura, but it is also very pertinent to an understanding of his conception of black life. Mailer continues, "I would go so far as to think it is my present and future work which will have the deepest influence of any work being done by an American novelist in these years."[51] He then suggests that "the reader who is curious to test my claims this instant is advised to turn to the pages of 'The White Negro.' " Mailer obviously considered this essay (first published in *Dissent* in 1957, later reprinted by City Lights Books, and again in *Advertisements for Myself*) to be a key statement of his philosophy and illustrative of his best work.

"The White Negro" had its origin in a statement Mailer made about southern resistance to school integration. His friend Lyle Stuart, editor of a monthly newspaper, had made a vaulted claim for the freedom and independence of the American press. Mailer responded with a wager. He would write a statement about the real reasons for resistance to integration. Lyle would publish it and then they would see if a major paper would dare to reprint it. Mailer wrote that whites resist integration and thus equality in the classroom because they secretly know that "the Negro already enjoys sensual superiority. So the white unconsciously feels that the balance has been kept, that the old arrangement was fair. The Negro had his sexual supremacy and the white had his white supremacy." Lyle published Mailer's statement, along with reactions he had requested from William Faulkner and other notables, but no other papers picked up the story. Faulkner's reply was a curt and damaging dismissal that stung Mailer deeply. Faulkner commented:

> I have heard this idea expressed several times during the last twenty years, though not before by a man.
> The others were ladies, northern or middle western ladies, usually around 40 or 45 years of age. I don't know what a psychiatrist would find in this.[52]

Mailer's ego could not allow the rebuff to go unchallenged. He called Faulkner a "timid man who has led a sheltered life" and had probably had most of his conversations with middle-aged ladies.

Even after his reply, Mailer still smarted from the sting of "a novelist who was to me a great writer." It was this feeling that drove Mailer to further clarify his ideas about black and white life, and thus to write "The White Negro." After finishing the essay, he came to sense that " 'The White Negro' is one of the best things I have done, and if it is difficult to read, it is also I think worth attention." In it can be found a "muted autobiography of the near-beat adventurer who was myself." Most of Mailer's critics have also underscored the importance to his ideology of this brief essay. Barry Leeds, for example, asserts that *Advertisements for Myself* seems to lie at the heart of the development of Mailer's ideas between the 1950s and the 1960s and that "The White Negro" is indisputably at the heart of *Advertisements*.[53]

Mailer opens his essay with a description of the physical and spiritual conditions of life in this country after World War II. It was an era of Eisenhower and prosperity, of Senator McCarthy and fearful conformity: "A stench of fear has come out of every pore of American life, and we suffer from a collective failure of nerve. The only courage, with rare exceptions, that we have been witness to, has been the isolated courage of isolated people." What follows is virtually

Mailer's manifesto. He describes the phenomenon that is occurring in the midst of American conformity — the appearance of an American Existentialist, — the hipster, who sees that his survival demands that he divorce himself from society and "exist without roots." The hipster's rebellion takes him on an "uncharted journey" into direct experience. Such a life will be fraught with danger but the alternative is the boredom and sickness of conformity. The hipster lives fully in the present, in an "enormous present" without past or future. He must marshall his courage and "gamble with his energies" and his life. As Mailer expresses it,

> The unstated essence of Hip, its psychopathic brilliance, quivers with the knowledge that new kinds of victories increase one's power for new kinds of perception; and defeats, the wrong kind of defeats, attack the body and imprison one's energy until one is jailed in the prison air of other people's habits, other people's defeats, boredom, quiet desperation and muted icy self-destroying rage. One is Hip or one is Square...one is a rebel or one conforms, one is a frontiersman in the Wild West of American night life, or else a square cell, trapped in the totalitarian tissues of American society.[54]

The language is forceful and impressive. It harkens back to the Thoreau of *Walden*, evoking one of his key phrases, "quiet desperation." The language is muscular and compelling. One senses Mailer's certainty and zeal in every phrase.

Now Mailer turns to black life and its influence on his emergent white heroes. He observes, categorically, that the "source of Hip is the Negro for he has been living on the margin between totalitarianism and democracy for two centuries." The existential quality of black life and of jazz have had penetrating influence on young white adventurers of the postwar generation, Mailer claims. The lengthy quote that follows expresses this central image and idea of "The White Negro." It also presents Mailer's most detailed portrait of black life during this period.

So no wonder that in certain cities of America, in New York of course, and New Orleans, in Chicago and San Francisco and Los Angeles, in such American cities as Paris and Mexico, D.F., this particular part of a generation was attracted to what the Negro had to offer. In such places as Greenwich Village, a ménage-à-trois was completed — the bohemian and the juvenile delinquent came face-to-face with the Negro, and the hipster was a fact in American life. If marijuana was the wedding ring, the child was the language of Hip for its argot gave expression to abstract states of feeling which all could share, at least all who were Hip. And in this wedding of the white and the black it was the Negro who brought the cultural dowry. Any Negro who wishes to live must live with danger from his first day, and no experience can ever be casual to him, no Negro can saunter down a street with any real certainty that violence will not visit him on his walk. The cameos of security for the average white: mother and the home, job and family, are not even a mockery to millions of Negroes; they are impossible. The Negro has the simplest of alternatives: live a life of constant humility or ever-threatening danger. In such a pass where paranoia is as vital to survival as blood, the Negro had stayed alive and begun to grow by following the need of his body where he could. Knowing in the cells of his existence that life was war, nothing but war, the Negro (all exceptions admitted) could rarely afford the sophisticated inhibitions of civilization, and so he kept for his survival the art of the primitive, he lived in the enormous present, he subsisted for his Saturday night kicks, relinquishing the pleasures of the mind for the more obligatory pleasures of the body, and in his music he gave voice to the character and quality of his existence, to his rage and the infinite variations of joy, lust, languor, growl, cramp, pinch, scream and despair of his orgasm. For jazz is orgasm, it is the music of orgasm, good orgasm and bad, and so it spoke across a nation, it had the communication of art even where it was watered, perverted, corrupted, and almost killed, it spoke in no matter what laundered popular way of instantaneous existential states to which some whites could respond, it was indeed a communication by art because it said, "I feel this, and now you do too."

So there was a new breed of adventurers, urban
adventruers who drifted out at night looking for action
with a black man's code to fit their facts. The hipster had
absorbed the existentialist synapses of the Negro, and for
practical purposes could be considered a white Negro.[55]

This passage reveals how dearly Mailer reveres black
culture, including the poverty, malnourishment, and job-
lessness that have characterized ghetto life. Mailer is not
being condescending; he believes these conditions are
acceptable because they toughen the body and temper the
soul. The white hipster has much to learn from black life if
he will but drop his pale existence and prowl the night
streets of urban America, seeking his Saturday night kicks.
Survival is the art of the primitive. Mailer believes that the
realities of being black in white America are a virtue in
disguise. They force upon one a greater sensitivity to
surroundings. Nothing is taken for granted. One is constantly
at the ready, committed to living and willing to act. The
degree of alertness to every aspect of living is what Mailer
finds so admirable in black life. Mailer makes no specific
references to place, organization, or individual; in fact he
refers only to "The Negro." One is reminded here of Ralph
Ellison's image (in *Shadow and Act*) of a black Gulliver,
trussed and staked and being swarmed over by thousands of
white pigmies observing every feature of his clothing and
body. There is in Mailer's essay only "The Negro" — one
great solitary figure representing all the blacks of urban
America.

James Baldwin expressed his dismay over Mailer's essay
in a now somewhat celebrated essay, "The Black Boy Looks
at the White Boy." It appeared originally in *Esquire* in 1961
and later in Baldwin's collection of essays, *Nobody Knows My
Name* (1963). Baldwin recalls here his furious resistance to
the title "The White Negro," and to the idea "that so antique
a vision of the blacks should, at this late hour, and in so
many borrowed heirlooms, be stepping off the A Train." It

was obvious to Baldwin that Mailer had a singular concept of blacks as sexually superior to whites. It would be silly and impertinent in this study to argue one side or the other of this assumption. The point is that Mailer does create a mass portrait of black sexuality. In doing so he denies individuality by placing a single idea about sex and race in front of the facts of individual lives. Baldwin also felt tired of challenging and correcting. He felt that few white writers really looked at black life or listened to their black friends because "they wanted their romance."

Baldwin observes, perhaps with some pleasure, that the black jazz musicians among whom he and Mailer sometimes found themselves

> did not for an instant consider him as being even remotely "hip" and Norman did not know this and I could not tell him. He never broke through to them, at least not as far as I know; and they were far too "hip," if that is the word I want, even to consider breaking through to him. They thought he was a real sweet ofay cat, but a little frantic."[56]

Despite the complex relationship that has existed between the two writers, this is a very damaging statement, if accepted as true. It deflates Mailer's claim for the hipster as a "White Negro." He is, instead, perhaps more a "real sweet ofay cat, but a little frantic." Of course, the term "white Negro" had to be a non sequitur from the start. Hipsters had a "reverter clause" on their new identity. They could always return to the mainstream of white life if driven to do so. Further, many blacks were forced by birth and racial identity to a desperate way of life that Mailer's so-called "white Negroes" chose to embrace. This creates two conflicting psychologies of living. It would be valuable to know how many black people would choose the danger and difficult circumstances that, Mailer claims, sharpen their reflexes and keep them at the cutting edge.

Baldwin also discusses his intermittent friendship with

Mailer in this essay. They first met in an apartment in Paris, "two lean cats, one white and one black." Like prizefighters, they circled and sparred with each other all that first evening. Mailer was more famous and could have pulled rank on Baldwin, but Baldwin's strength lay in the fact that "I was black and knew more of the periphery he so helplessly maligns in "The White Negro" than he could ever hope to know." He sensed that Mailer wanted to know him as much as he wanted to know Mailer, but one of the barriers between them was "that myth of the sexuality of the Negroes which Norman, like so many others, refuses to give up." Baldwin detested having to play the "noble savage" or any other role before Mailer, because "all roles are dangerous. The world tends to trap and immobilize you in the role you play."[57]

Eldridge Cleaver also comments on "The White Negro" and Baldwin's objections in his essay "Notes on a Native Son," from *Soul on Ice* (1968). Cleaver's unflagging support of Mailer, in the late sixties, helps one perceive the degree that "The White Negro" anticipated black thinking of a decade later. Cleaver praises the essay as "prophetic and penetrating in its understanding of the psychology involved in the accelerating confrontation of black and white in America."[58] He considers the essay "one of the few gravely important expressions of our time" and Baldwin's dismissal of it a "literary crime."

Mailer and Cleaver similarly reduce and simplify human nature to binary alternatives. Mailer allows that one is either hip or square. Cleaver declares in *Soul on Ice* that white males are "Omnipotent Administrators" and black males are "Supermasculine Menials." He sees a world of heads separated from bodies in which the dominating white culture has divorced itself from its body as thoroughly as it has denied the black man his mind. Both Cleaver and Mailer are reformers and both reduce the world to allegorical terms so that the truth in essential relationships may be clearly seen. In doing so they find acceptable a very limited range of male and female behavior and attack or ignore images that do not conform. Consequently, Mailer seems compelled to depict blacks as urban hipsters living in the zone of danger.

Thus "The White Negro" not only evokes strongly conflicting responses from two important black writers, but occasions important statements that reveal their fundamental differences. Although Baldwin's sexual revolt and political detachment no doubt estranged him from Cleaver and other black writers of the late sixties, his objections to Mailer's narrow conception of "black life" certainly ring with some accuracy.[60] But at the same time one can understand Cleaver's insistence on emphasizing heroic portraits of black men and women and the reunification of the "black mind and body."

With *An American Dream* one jumps seven years in Mailer's art to find a much more sophisticated presentation of the ideas initially expressed in "The White Negro." The reader also encounters Shago Martin, Mailer's first and only black character of real dimension. At first glance Shago Martin seems to be very much what one might expect from Mailer: a fictionalized portrait of one of those stereotyped blacks who never actually appear in "The White Negro." It must have been Mailer's initial strategy to write a novel that would dramatize his ideas in "The White Negro." He would bring together a white hipster, his black counterpart, a woman or two, and the various other ingredients described in his essay in order to illustrate the rites-of-passage of a white conformist into a Maileresque hero. Later the reader will see how Mailer added levels of complexity to his black character, thus creating a very individual portrait from what could have been merely an expression of his theoretical conceptions of black life.

Shago Martin is a popular black singer. In fact, he is the most popular black singer in America. He is also a "Prince" and "Lord of Harlem." The white protagonist Stephen Rojack describes Shago's entrance this way: "An elegant

Negro with a skin dark as midnight was standing there. He
looked at the robe I was wearing."[61] Shago has let himself
into Cherry's apartment, as is his custom, only to find a white
man, Stephen Rojack, sitting there with his girl and wearing
his robe. He lingers in the doorway for a moment, and in his
left hand he holds a furled umbrella. Shago Martin's first
words are not unexpectedly, "Get dressed. Get your white
ass out of here."

Stephen feels he has known Shago before this awkward
encounter, because he has seen Shago's face so many times
on record jackets and in a movie or two about jazz musicians.
"A handsome face, thin and arrogant, a mask," he thinks.
Stephen's wife, Deborah, considered Shago the most attractive
man in America, but Deborah is dead now, murdered by
Stephen earlier this same day. Rojack has also heard Shago
sing at the Latin Quarter and the Copacabana. It was said
that Shago came out of one of the worst gangs in Harlem. He
is popular, enormously good-looking, yet independent and
indifferent to his popularity.

If anything, Shago's talent was too extreme. There was
nothing stereotyped about it. It did not suggest "that the
nicest affair of the year was about to start," and it did not
evoke "landscapes in Jamaica, of mangoes, honey and a
breast beneath the moon." Shago's music gave you some of
that, but

> "there were snakes in his tropical garden, and a wild pig
> was off in the wilderness with a rip in its flank from the
> teeth of a puma, he gave you a world of odd wild cries, and
> imprisoned it to something complex in his style, some
> irony, some sense of control, some sense of the way every-
> thing is brought back at last under control. And he had a
> beat which went right through your ear into your body, it
> was cruel, it was perfect, it gave promise of teaching a
> paralytic to walk." (182)

Rojack's description reveals the complexity of Martin's

musical style and of his personality. He is a musician for more than money and reputation; his music is self-expression. As his personality evolves, his music "persisted in shifting." Some of his more experimental music sounded at first "like a clash of hysterias." But there is more to Shago even than this: Mailer finally tells his reader that "he was like a mind racing between separate madnesses." The alternating madnesses are white society, which would have cannibalized him, and the street environment of Harlem and heroin, which finally kills him. Still, hysteria did not dominate his music, although it found expression in it. To those who really listened, "Shago Martin's beat was always harder, faster, or a hesitation slower than the reflex of your ear, but you were glowing when he was done, the ear felt good, you had been dominated by a champion" (182).

As he enters the apartment Shago Martin also recognizes Stephen Rojack, for he has seen the white man's television program and he has probably heard by now of Stephen's questioning in his wife's apparent suicide. Stephen's wife is the socialite and heiress, Deborah Kelly Rojack. In fact, Shago has been informed he is to take over the television time formerly assigned to Rojack. (Coincidence follows coincidence in *An American Dream*). Shago might also recall Stephen's term as a congressman from New York and some of his credentials: Phi Beta Kappa and *summa cum laude* from Harvard, war hero, friend of President Kennedy (they double-dated once), author, and a professor of existential psychology at a New York university. Rojack is, in short, Mailer's "white Negro" in transition from "square" to "hip."

When Stephen Rojack was in active pursuit of success and power, he fell for Deborah; her father was one of the wealthiest, most influential men in America. He needed Barney Kelly's money and influence to get elected and wield the political power he craved. Although he thought he would use this power to good purpose, he had, Mailer implies, established a pact with the devil. He had, without realizing it, chosen a cowardly and self-destructive route to power. In this sense, the novel is a morality play in which Barney Kelly is cast as the devil, and St. Stephen is a good man sorely tempted. He has lived in the very house of the devil and has been married to his daughter for nine years. His courage and will to act have been shorn. Stephen's father-in-law controls people by encouraging them to conform, to submit, and to squander their talents. Rojack slowly comes to realize he must revolt in order to believe in himself.

Mailer's theology centers on a movement toward individual action and self-reliance. As Robert Solataroff puts it, *An American Dream* is "one man's attempts to strengthen his being against many of those forces in America which might seek to weaken it — perversity, war, police, mafia, politics, mass media, racial terror, high society, big business." Rojack's murder of his wife and later the confrontation with her father are essential to his quest for authenticity. He risks life and risks dying to be reborn. This fictional rendering of Mailer's ontology takes his autobiographical hero, as Solataroff expresses it, into many "demonic areas of American life and his own psyche."[62]

Time stops for Stephen Rojack as he watches Shago Martin standing in the doorway before him. It is like the meeting of doubles, or of two elements destined to come together to form a whole. Both look each other over, size each other up. It is a classic stand-off. Stephen senses that "a wind came off him, a poisonous snake of mood which entered my lungs like marijuana, and time began to slow." It is a frozen instant, "like that hesitation before the roller coaster drops."

Here is an interesting variation on the ménage-à-trois Mailer describes in "The White Negro." In the lengthy passage from "The White Negro" quoted earlier, Mailer describes a "wedding of the white and the black" in which the white juvenile delinquent and the bohemian "came face-to-face with the Negro" and "the hipster was a fact in American life." Mailer describes it as a marriage to which the black brought the cultural dowry, "marijuana was the wedding ring," and "the child was the language of hip" that gave them expression. It appears significant that Mailer describes this relationship of blacks and whites as a "wedding." This is as fraternal and idyllic a rendition of the "natural" tale as one will find; it is a union of the two forces in holy matrimony. One is reminded of the idyllic relationships of Alexander Henry and the Indian named Wawatam (see Chapter 1), and of Ike and Sam Fathers in Faulkner's "The Bear." But the relationship in *An American Dream* varies from that described in "The White Negro," for the triangle now involves Cherry, a very beautiful, blond, white singer who lived with Shago and has now pledged herself to Stephen. Rojack is clearly the bridegroom and Cherry his bride. Shago, completing the triangle, is an amalgamation of priest, rival lover, and father of the bride. He brings the hashish that is to be their wedding ring, but he is so "stoned" that they are frightened and refuse to smoke with him. He also brings "the gift of tongues," a spirit-laden umbrella, and the power of magic, which he leaves as wedding gifts.

The language Mailer uses to describe Shago Martin is heavy with primitive reference. Shago's breath carries "a poisonous snake of mood," and his switchblade opens from his palm "like a snake's tongue." His voice conveys images of "a world of odd wild cries." His eyes dart "like cockroaches under the flare of lights." Shago is a tribal priest come down from Harlem to test the strength and nerve of Stephen Rojack, and if he is ready, to complete the double ceremony of initiation and marriage to the girl chosen and "prepared" for him. All this would seem too fanciful an interpretation were it not for the wedding imagery Mailer uses in "The White Negro" and the very obvious allegory he develops in this novel. As is so typical of characters drawn in the natural mode, Shago tests and then inducts Rojack into a new world, a ceremony vividly reminiscent of Sam Father's initiation of Ike McCaslin into the realm of the wilderness. For both Ike and Stephen, this is the beginning of a new way of life and transformed vision of the world.

It is important to emphasize that the movement of this novel is from the civilized to the primitive, from Manhattan to the jungle of Yucatán; Stephen's progress is from reason to intuition and magic. The Shago Martin chapter is titled "A Votive is Prepared," further suggesting the black man's function in Stephen's education. Stephen is being prepared for combat with his father-in-law, the devil. It is not surprising, then, that Mailer turns to tribal ritual in shaping this crucial scene. Mailer seems particularly inclined to "homeopathic magic," the ancient principle of magic based on the conviction in countless ancient societies that "like produces like."[63] In fact, this principle of magic helps explain "The White Negro" itself. From a magical standpoint, whites can best learn to be like blacks by symbolically becoming "black." Homeopathy is a belief in intrinsic magical relationships between objects. Among tribal peoples sexual intercourse at the time of planting does not merely symbolize fertility. According to Sir James Frazer, it is believed to engender plant fertility magically, as leaping over a newly planted field will produce hight-growing crops. Tribal peoples often wear the skin of an animal they wish to emulate. In this sense, whites who wish to become "hip" must follow if not get inside the skin of their black counterparts, according to Mailer's tribal mysticism. Thus the otherwise objectionable phrase "white Negro" is understandable as an expression of homeopathic magic.

It is no coincidence that Mailer has Stephen wearing Shago's robe as the black man enters. Wearing his robe is like wearing his skin, and Stephen is unconsciously becoming Shago Martin. Stephen is also learning, as he says, what love is all about. He is learning to love and to achieve "apocalyptic orgasm" with a woman who has been opened to loving by a black man. As Frazer would explain it, "like produces like." Stephen and Cherry have been selected for "sacred marriage." Shago has determined Cherry's worthiness and in the scene that follows he determines Stephen's suitability. He stands before Rojack "like a priest with a candle," looking down at the blade of his knife. The blade poses castration, a sufficient threat to determine Rojack's courage. But Stephen casually stands his ground, offering Shago a cigarette. "I be damn," Shago declares to Cherry, "you got yourself a stud who can stand," and later, as if to encourage the initiate, he declares, "This cat's got valour."

The fight that follows suggests a confrontation with the "ally" that often takes place in tribal initiation ceremonies. The priest or ally tests the initiate's strength and skill. Wrestling with the ally is presumably the occasion during which magic passes from one to the other, as their bodies make contact. Stephen has been singled out, Mailer suggests, not just for initiation into the tribe (usually a rite closer to puberty) but for special or sacred knowledge and sacred marriage. After the fight Stephen will be as if born anew. Armed with knowledge and power, and the "votive" prepared, he will vow to confront Barney Kelly.

The great powers Shago possesses and Stephen does not are intuitive magic and the "gift of tongues." A priest possessing the magic of language, Shago launches into a high, drug-speeded monologue that is variously a demonstration of his verbal skill, a wedding aria, and an agonizing self-confession of weakness and despair. It ends with insults to the groom so stinging that they force him to action.

At first Shago congratulates Stephen and Cherry on their newfound love, for it is obvious he has lost Cherry: "If I got to lose, I got to lose to a square with heart." Then he shares the revelation about Stephen and Deborah that has come to him. He had been working his way up from small jazz clubs in Harlem, then in the Village, and finally to places like the Copa and the Latin Quarter. He was becoming well known and making some money. His revelation occurred one night when Stephen and his former wife sat in the front row listening to him. She had been trying to get Shago to play at a charity ball. "Why I knew your wife was a society bitch," exclaims Shago. "That's a *bitch!* I knew what she was promising, all that White House jazz, mow my grass, black boy, you're so sexy — think I like to pass that up?" (189). But, he continues, "I took one look at your wife and I gave it up." He saw Deborah sitting there, eyeing him like a sophisticated cannibal. He was ready to sell his origin and culture to become a black darling of white society until he saw her in the front row, "eating me, man I could feel the marrow oozing from my bones, a cannibal." He saw in Deborah the "face of the Devil." This helps explain the "clash of hysterias" and the "mind racing between separate madnesses" Rojack sometimes hears in Shago's tortured music. It is the music of his soul in agony. Even though Shago has returned to playing small jazz clubs and to relative oblivion, he is still estranged from black life. (" I'm cut off from my own lines." "I'm a white man now.")

Then Shago displays his "gift of tongues," revealing both his considerable talent and his great despair:

> "Cause I can do the tongues, all that cosmopolitan *dreck*, bit of French, bit of Texas, *soupcon* of Oxford jazz — I promise you," he interpolated with a perfect London voice, "that we'll have masses of fun and be happy as a clam, why," he said, snapping his fingers, "I can pick up on the German, Chinese, Russian (*Tovarich,* mother-fucker) I can do a piece of each little bit, St. Nicholas Avenue *upper* nigger, Jamaican, Japanese, Javanese, high yaller sass — I just call on my adenoids, my fat lips and tonsils, *waaaaah,* I can do *grande dame,* anything from a gasbag to Tallulah Bankhead, "Out, you pederast," it's all shit, man, except for the way I use it cause I let each accent pick its note, every tongue on a private note, when I sing it's a congregation of tongues, that's the spook in my music, that's why they got to buy me big or not at all, I'm not intimate, I'm Elizabethan, a chorus, dig?" (190)

His "gift of tongues" helps him recreate the world with words and thus bring it under his control, reshaping it according to his needs. During Shago's monologue of word magic Stephen and Cherry seem immobilized, imprisoned by the effect his speech. His language is the child, the off-spring of the ménage-à-trois. The "language of hip" is a reality in itself, giving "expression to abstract states of feeling that all could share, at least all who were hip." But Shago has squandered this talent, as he has his musical genius. His "gift of tongues" has deteriorated to a "congrega-tion of tongues" suitable for clever imitations to please sophisticated white audiences.

During this scene Shago comes alive as a character in his own right; he is no longer a functionary, serving to advance Mailer's design for his white characters. Mailer has paused significantly to develop the character of Shago, to let him speak with his "gift of tongues," and thus to reveal the complexity of his life and anguish of his soul. He is a tragic figure, a black man who perceived too late to save himself that he was engaged in the white devil's work.

Shago at last turns the venom of his tongue to Rojack, playing the dozens, (a game of insults), and finally goading him to attack. He mentions various men Deborah has slept with and speculates that she kept Rojack around to lick her feet. Shago dares to turn his back to Rojack, and at that instant, in a rage of red, Stephen grabs him. Mailer's choice of words suggests the various levels on which this skirmish takes place: "I took him from behind, my arms about his waist, hefted him in the air, and slammed him to the floor so hard his legs went, and we ended with Shago in a sitting position, and me behind him on my knees, my arms choking the air from his chest as I lifted him up and smashed him down, and lifted him up and smashed him down again" (192).

As Howard Harper, Jr. has suggested in *Desperate Faith* (1967), there is some suggestion of rape or attempted rape in this scene. Rojack picks Shago up from behind and slams him down perhaps twenty times. During this scene Shago yells, "Let me go I'll kill you, bugger," and twice yells at Rojack, "Up your ass, Mother Fuck." Rojack finally "manhandles" him to the door and is nearly overcome by "a smell of full nearness as if we'd been in bed for an hour." Of course this is strange language, taken literally, with which to depict a struggle between rival lovers. Mailer presumably has in mind suggesting a complex relationship in which both the lurking fantasy of homosexual love and the humiliation of rape occur to Martin and Rojack. They are enraged by, yet strongly attracted to each other.

The fight continues out into the hall and down two flights of stairs. At the end Shago is physically defeated but remains the master of language, alternating between threats, puns, and compliments. Rojack has won the last direct challenge from Shago, and the black "priest" offers his blessing to the lovers. " 'Tell you something, man, I don't hate. Never. That's it. . . . Tell Cherry, her and you, I wish you luck.' " Stephen has had two powerful advantages in this confrontation with his rival. He has been wearing Shago's robe throughout the scene, and in somewhat cowardly fashion, he attacks Shago from behind. But Shago is somewhere between a mortal and a shaman. He loses graciously, for that is part of his function. He has tested the mettle of this couple and passes his mantle (the robe) and his blessing on to them, a powerful ally to have on their side. He also leaves his umbrella behind, intentionally one presumes — and Cherry presents it to Stephen. " 'Now you got a stick,' she said." Stephen is also the first man who has enabled Cherry to experience orgasm (" 'Never before . . . Stephen, when a man was within me' "), and the furled umbrella is a tribute to his sexual accomplishment. Since "apocalyptic orgasm" such as they achieved is essential to Mailer's blacks and hipsters, Stephen is a sexual hero as well.

Combative power and sexual superiority he has won, but

there is another dimension to Shago's power that Stephen will have to realize. In a touching tribute to Martin, Cherry says, " 'Shago was the only man I ever knew who could make something in me turn over when he came into a room. I don't know if I'll ever feel that again. I think you get that only with one man' " (198).

Thus Stephen Rojack leaves Cherry's apartment, a man transformed. His victory and the orgasm he experienced with Cherry have been profoundly liberating and visionary. It is perhaps, as Tony Tanner has suggested, his "re-established contact with the secret source of life."[64] He has also been relying more and more on non-rational ways of knowing and influencing events. He communes with the moon, uses mental telepathy to entice Cherry and hypnosis to ward off a rival. Now he is also armed with the magic bequeathed him by Shago, including the "gift of tongues," which speaks to him through the umbrella. Stephen makes hi way uptown to the Waldorf and Barney Kelly's suite on the thirtieth floor. Stephen has sensed all day that he will have to confront and perhaps defeat his father-in-law. Barney will sense that Stephen has killed Deborah and that it is total war.

With subtlety and patience, Kelly tries to subdue Rojack, but Stephen is internally calm and untempted. Soon he realizes that he will have to walk the narrow parapet around the Kelly apartment; he will have to walk it twice, in order to free himself from this man, his daughter, and their influence. The novel operates principally on the allegorical level at this point. Clearly, Stephen is Mailer's emerging existential hero, and the parapet is, as Tony Tanner has pointed out, the precarious balancing edge between all extremes. Rojack "has to prove he can negotiate the edge where the worlds meet — capitulating neither to a political nor to a demonizing ordering of reality, avoiding the traps of social architecture and the chaotic dissolutions of the pre-social and the sub-social dark."[65] Rojack has to keep his balance to win his

liberation from these opposed worlds, as represented by
Shago and by Kelly. When Kelly sees that Rojack will
successfully negotiate the parapet, he lunges with Shago's
umbrella, trying to push Stephen off. Stephen grabs the
umbrella, strikes Kelly down, and tosses it away.

In "The White Negro" Mailer commented that the twentieth
century is very exciting "for its tendency to reduce all of life
to its ultimate alternatives." Whether this is true or not,
Mailer certainly relishes reducing life to simple alternatives.
In his work there is a fairly continuous schematizing of life
into opposed pairs. Tony Tanner describes Mailer as
continually "postulating pairs of opposed extremes — assassins
and victims; conformists and outlaws; the black magician
versus the good artist; love and death; being and nothingness;
cannibals and Christians — and finally God and the Devil."[66]
Mailer's hipster-as-hero bravely battles the power brokers,
whose influence and control grow like the malignancy of
cancer through society. Only a few individuals and groups
have the wisdom to see the deadening of life and the
strength to combat it. Blacks have it, and so do hipsters. In
Mailer's world-view, God and the Devil are locked into a
metaphysical battle for control of life. God represents
existential living and the Devil is a force whose "joy is to
waste substance." It is an awesomely allegorical world. Both
Stephen and Shago discover this metaphysical battle and
find that they have been on the wrong side. Shago learns too
late and is destroyed in his struggle with the Devil, and
Stephen nearly plunges off the parapet to his death. Stephen's
balancing act seems to represent the necessary condition for
Mailer's heroes. They must balance between too much form
and formlessness, between empiricism and magic, between
tower and chasm. Stephen survives, though barely, his
confrontation with Kelly, only to find that Shago, in his
weakened condition, has been killed, and that Cherry has
been mistakenly killed by one of Shago's friends. Heartbroken, Rojack leaves New York, still weak and vulnerable,

but also powerfully armed. He is, for Mailer, a prototype, an evolutionary human being searching for a suitable environment.

Although Mailer's more recent novel *Why Are We In Vietnam?* (1967) does not contain black characters, it incorporates Shago Martin's "gift of tongues." The hero and narrator of this novel is Ranald Jethroe, a precocious sixteen-year-old from Dallas who imagines himself a cosmic disc jockey. When he is high on pot, "D.J.," as he is called, seems to gain access to the verbal magic of Shago Martin. It is as if Shago is still alive, a bedridden, crippled, Harlem genius, unable to speak except through the voice of Mailer's tough teenager. Through the "gift of tongues" D.J. also gives voice to, among others, an army top sergeant, a Hell's Angel, and a southern deputy sheriff. It appears that Mailer's teenage hipster and his pal, Tex Hyde, have become "white Negroes" without having to walk the parapet's knife edge or roam the desperate streets of Harlem. But like Mailer's blacks and white hipsters, they demonstrate by the end of the novel, the importance of recapturing courage, of staying open to adventure, of living on the knife edge of experience. With this novel one significant alteration of the old "white Negro" formula seems apparent: whites no longer need to confront or even encounter blacks to become existential heroes. Mailer seems to be moving away from the "hipster" as a basis for his heroes.

Mailer has quite consistently portrayed blacks as wise and sophisticated primitives, and his more recent essays in *Existential Errands* (1971) reveal no exception to this belief. Mailer's statements about black life appear to be totally absent of intentional pejorative. He honestly believes that blacks are stronger than whites, quicker in reflexes, more existential, more intuitive, better at sex, healthier, that they have superior psychic powers and a superior culture. What other white writer has so thoroughly and enthusiastically embraced black life in America? In fact, Mailer often seems to have abandoned hope for white America and for blacks who insist upon being merely "Negroes." Mailer continues to believe in those occasional white adventurers like Stephen Rojack, who can learn aliveness from black culture and point the way for other whites to follow.

More recently, Mailer has provided a major black portrait in his account of the Muhammad Ali/George Foreman fight held in Zaire (*The Fight*, 1975). Mailer first records his growing admiration for Ali in an article assembled by the editors of *Partisan Review* (Summer 1967) titled "In Clay's Corner." Mailer is, interestingly enough, the only writer interviewed sensitive enough to Ali's wishes to at least use his new name as well as his old. In his assault on the boxing officials who stripped Muhammad Ali of his heavyweight title, Mailer calls Ali "the most interesting original talented and artistic fighter to come along in at least a decade." Not unlike Shago Martin, Ali is for Mailer one of those rare bursts of genius who are potentially revolutionary if their talents are not squandered or diverted. Mailer could see already that Ali was "bringing a revolution to the theory of boxing." In this brief article Mailer reveals his more-than-passing interest in Ali, commenting, "I could write a book about Cassius," which, of course, he does.

For Mailer, an extraordinary athlete is invariably an extraordinary man. Even in the *Partisan Review* article Mailer enunciates his admiration of greatness and dislike of mediocrity among both boxers and writers. This connection is further developed in *The Fight*. The only white character of consequence in the book is Mailer himself. The scene has shifted from New York to the heart of Africa. What Mailer records in Zaire is anything but a *Heart of Darkness;* round by round he convinces himself and his readers of the strategy, control, and brilliance of Ali in his victory. After allowing himself to be backed into the ropes for seven rounds, dancing on the ropes, dodging Foreman's punches and jabbing swiftly with his own, Ali finally attacks in the eighth.

Mailer describes the knockout blow at the end of the eighth: "Then a big projectile exactly the size of a fist in a glove drove into the middle of Foreman's mind, the best punch of the startled night, the blow Ali saved for a career" (169). Back in America, after the fight, many were claiming that the fight was fixed. "The fight was fixed. Yes. So was *The Night Watch* and *Portrait of the Artist As a Young Man*," Mailer asserts, defending his champion.

Mailer went to Zaire, it is probably fair to say, himself a battler and a champ without title, to observe firsthand and pay homage to a peer. After the fight and a minor skirmish of his own, Mailer gains entrance to Ali's dressing room, but finds himself humbled, desiring to "pay his respects" and "simple tribute," rather than capitalize on the opportunity for an exclusive interview. Although Mailer's portraits of Ali and Foreman deserve much more detailed consideration than they receive here, suffice it to say that Mailer's initial interest in Ali turns into admiration and finally awe. (Ali, who so often put words to Mailer's feelings, commented, as they jogged together days before the fight, "It'll be a great experience for you remembering that you ran with the Champion.") There is no trace of the fear and ambivalence Mailer's white hero, Stephen Rojack, felt toward Shago Martin. (After his successful fight with Martin, Rojack revealed that "some hard-lodged boulder of fear I had always felt with Negroes was in the bumping, elbow-busting...crash of sound as he went barreling down...my terror going with him.")[67] Perhaps the difference is that Mailer is on the right side and a noncombatant as well, and thus can observe Ali's courage, daring, and brilliance with detached appreciation. But Ali's victory underscores the point that in fiction Mailer is willing to sacrifice his blacks, once his white characters have drawn from the black strength and talent. What role would Mailer assign to Muhammad Ali as a character in one of his novels?

Mailer's fictional blacks are primitives with natural-born

talents who are as willing to give of their magic, their strength, their sexual potency, as they are willing to teach, to initiate, to be sacrificed for the good of his white characters. What is most unsettling about "The White Negro" and the other works discussed here is the one-sidedness of the proposition. Mailer has always been more interested in an intellectual conception of black life than in blacks themselves. Blacks are his illustrations and teaching points — insofar as they substantiate his ideas. Regrettably, he fights conformity and totalitarianism with an artistic totalitarianism of his own. In his essays there is no room for less than militant and less than super-masculine blacks. Mailer is, as Joyce Carol Oates says, "so dangerous a visionary," precisely because he is willing to sacrifice individuality to his concepts.[68]

But Mailer the fiction writer is not entirely hidebound by the totalitarianism of Mailer the philosopher and essayist. His Shago Martin, while surely an illustration of the necessary relationship of blacks to his emerging "white Negroes," is distinctly his own man. One may object to the various functions he performs as priest, sexual rival, and sacrificial lover, but nearly all Mailer's characters function symbolically. Like Sam Fathers, he teaches what he knows, tests and challenges, certifies Rojack's completion of the rites-of-passage, gives him various magical powers, and then, like Sam, dies a mystical death off-stage, his mission completed. His mission is the education of a white man — not the living out of his own difficult, perhaps impossible life. Yet along with these objections it must be said that Mailer has invested time and effort in fleshing out Shago's character, in perfecting his "gift of tongues," and in revealing his discovery about the Devil's work. Shago is, at this level, distinctly a character in his own right. He grows in power and dimension, a complex and tortured black individual.

KURT VONNEGUT, JR.

Kurt Vonnegut's third novel, *Cat's Cradle* (1965), can be read as a satire on black stereotypes by white writers. Vonnegut's protagonist, a black Caribbean named Bokonon, is a self-proclaimed guru and spiritual leader to the people of his island. He might appear, on the surface, to be another black natural who guides, instructs, and initiates the white folks — a Sam Fathers or Shago Martin transported to the Caribbean. But such is not the case, for Vonnegut carefully and playfully avoids the various temptations and stereotypes of the natural mode. Vonnegut's other significant black character is Mona Aamons Monzano, a "morgrel modonna" and "natural erotic symbol" of the island. Here again one might expect a portrait of a young black woman who is a natural at sex. However, Vonnegut plays with these familiar types, often seeming to parody the very conventions of black primitivism as he does so.

Bokonon is not only spiritual leader of the natives who inhabit San Lorenzo island, but he is the founder of a religion called Bokononism. Like O'Neill's Brutus Jones, Bokonon has seen much of the world. He has learned about religion, wealth, and war, and as with Brutus he is cast ashore on a tropical island where he quickly establishes a new society. But Bokonon has come to some very different conclusions about haman values, and thus creates a radically different society. Vonnegut's handling of Bokonon is in striking contrast to the treatment of black portraits by writers already considered. Bokonon emerges as a thoroughly complex figure, brilliant in his insight into human nature, as well as comic and compassionate.

Vonnegut writes that Bokonon was born in 1891 and that "he was a Negro, born an Episcopalian and a British subject on the island of Tobago."[69] Christened Lionel Boyd Johnson (sounding painfully like the name of a former president), he was the youngest of six children in a wealthy family on

Tobago. Bokonon's grandfather found a quarter of a million dollars in buried pirate treasure, presumably the treasure of Blackbeard. Unlike Brutus Jones, Bokonon grew up in a family of affluence and was not particularly interested in accumulating wealth or in financial revenge. In 1911 he set sail, alone, for London on a family sloop named "Lady's Slipper." He continued his education at the London School of Economics, but this was interrupted by World War I. "He enlisted in the infantry, fought with distinction, was commissioned in the field, and mentioned four times in dispatches," writes Vonnegut (92). Discharged toward the end of the war, he set sail for home.

The adventures that follow are too numerous even to summarize. Yet during all these events Johnson was growing in the "conviction that something was trying to get him somewhere for some reason" (92). Several years later Johnson and an American Marine deserter, a white man named Earl McCabe, were shipwrecked on the rocky shore of San Lorenzo. Convinced that it was their fate to be cast up, naked, upon this unfamiliar island, the two decided to let the adventure run its course. Johnson felt that he was being reborn as he crawled from the sea and was given his new name, "Bokonon," by the islanders. It is the closest San Lorenzan dialect comes to saying "Johnson."

Thus began the partnership of McCabe and Bokonon. Declaring that they were taking over the island, they met little opposition from the native government or the American firm, Castle Sugar. They dreamed of making San Lorenzo a utopia. McCabe began overhauling the economy and laws; Bokonon designed a new religion. They worked against great odds, for, as Vonnegut puts it, "It had as dense a population as could be found anywhere, India and China not excluded. There were four hundred and fifty inhabitants for each uninhabitable square mile" (113). As the island's self-declared holy man, Bokonon penned a book of calypsos that, in simplified and entertaining form, carried the central ideas of his new religion.

> I wanted all things
> To seem to make some sense,
> So we all could be happy, yes,
> Instead of tense.
> And I made up lies
> So that they all fit nice,
> And I made this sad world
> A par-a-dise. (109)

Bokonon must have been overwhelmed by the endless presence of human poverty and misery, despite the declarations, charters, and constitutions proclaiming a better life for mankind. Under Ghandi's influence he became convinced that even the most desirable human goals do not justify violent, dehumanizing methods.

While in England, Bokonon had taken a muscle-building course from none other than Charles Atlas. Atlas taught him "Dynamic Tension," an exercise system that works on the principle that superior body conditioning results from pitting one set of muscles against another. Thus Bokonon's religious and human philosophies are pitted against a government and legal system designed by McCabe to be absolutely terrifying. But with McCabe's successor, "Papa" Monzano, the "good lie" of opposing forces became a serious opposition. At first "the hook" (for impaling criminals) was merely symbolic. But Bokonon did not anticipate that Monzano would take his power seriously, declaring the island religion illegal and Bokonon himself a public enemy.

The only thing sacred to Bokononists is man. And the most important activities in their lives are "fishing, fornication and *boko-maru*." Even though *boko-maru* is officially outlawed, everyone practices it in secret. It is a ceremony for the "mingling of awareness" between two Bokononists, by pressing the soles of the feet together. The narrator of the novel, a young American writer named Jonah, describes it like this:

"We Bokononists believe that it is impossible to be sole-to-sole with another person without loving the person, provided the feet of both persons are clean and nicely tended. The basis of the foot ceremony is this Calypso:

We will touch our feet, yes,
Yes, for all we're worth,
And we will love each other, yes,
Yes, like we love our Mother Earth." (132)

Bokonon's "dynamic tension" with "Papa" Monzano becomes gradually more precarious for the black holy man. In the printed text of Vonnegut's screen play for National Educational Television [*Between Time and Timbuktu* (1972)], one sees even more of this deteriorating relationship. Bokonon explains:

"No one was supposed to be killed. It was all threats and rumors. And then...the president and I drifted apart.... He was my best friend. We made a play, a work of art, of our life on the island. He would play the cruel tyrant in the city, and I the gentle holy man in the forest. It was an innocent make-believe — to distract the people from their miserable existence."[70]

Bokonon had believed the outlawing of his religion would give it "more zest, more tang." And of course it did, for a time. Bokonon's painful conclusion is that "you have to be very careful what you pretend to be...because one day you may wake up to find that's what you are."[71] Readers of Vonnegut's novels will perhaps recognize this line as a variation on one of two morals Vonnegut announces at the opening of his third novel, *Mother Night* (1961): "We are what we pretend to be, so we must be careful about what we pretend to be." This repetition is in itself evidence of the thematic consistency of Vonnegut's art. He manages through such repetitions of character and ideas to convey the intricate interrelationship of all his novels. They are like points in an elaborate string sculpture or cat's cradle. To touch one of his novels is, Vonnegut wants one to sense, to touch all of them. The string sculpture and Vonnegut's interrelated fiction may also be his expression of the ecosystem. A rupture or violent alteration at one point may eventually affect the entire chain of life.

Thus, a single "seed" of ice-nine accidentally touching the ocean at San Lorenzo freezes the world to death at the conclusion of *Cat's Cradle*. Ice-nine is a super weapon developed by a playfully absent-minded researcher named Dr. Felix Hoenikker, the "father" of the A-Bomb. Since this hybrid ice freezes at 114.4 degrees Fahrenheit, a single chip could freeze the waters of the world and bring to an end nearly all life on the planet. Thus, the primary "dynamic tension" of *Cat's Cradle* operates between Hoenikkerism and Bokononism, between ice-nine and *boko-maru*. While the one is a seed of death, the other is the gentle touching of flesh and commingling of souls. As in nearly all of Vonnegut's fiction, the deadly serious and the comic are brought into dynamic tension here. Although Vonnegut does not quite reduce this dialectic to the resolution "make love not war" — easily he could have. As with the *boko-maru*, Vonnegut indulges in many comic effects, such as Bokonon's amusing and simplistic calypsos, but he never does this at Bokonon's expense.

Dr. Hoenikker was a brilliant scientist who devoted his life to "pure research" at the General Forge and Foundry Company in Ilium, New York. Vonnegut clearly implies there is no such thing as pure research. Or, he believes, research is as pure as an atomic bomb, as pure as a crystal of ice-nine. Hoenikker's midget son, Newt, recalls that his father was "one of the best-protected human beings who ever lived. People couldn't get at him because he just wasn't interested in people" (22). Like Bokonon, then, Dr. Hoenikker stayed in hiding, but his hiding was from human contact. "Ah, God, what an ugly city Ilium is," observes Jonah, narrator of the novel. And Ilium is no worse than any other American city, in Vonnegut's eyes. It is ugly because of its pursuit of the abstractions of beauty and "the good life." The only things sacred to San Lorenzans are people: the only things sacred to America, in Vonnegut's novels, are progress and a high standard of living. Vonnegut and his narrator, Jonah, are clearly in sympathy with the black citizens of San Lorenzo and with their elusive mentor Bokonon.

Vonnegut's only black American in the novel is a "small ancient Negro" named Lyman Enders Knowles, an elevator operator at the General Forge and Foundry in Ilium. Knowles is a good illustration of Vonnegut's masterful ability to give life and complexity even to his walk-on characters. Knowles addresses his captive audience before he pushes the button. " 'Hello, fellow anthropoids and lily pads and paddlewheels,' " he says to Jonah and Miss Faust (a secretary who has presumably made a pact with her employer, the Devil) as they enter his elevator. Knowles is reminiscent of the "yam man" and several other black characters in Ralph Ellison's *Invisible Man* who work and survive within white society because they manage to see with clarity and spread their wisdom to others. Lyman Enders Knowles tells Jonah:

> "This here's a *re*-search laboratory. *Re*-search means *look again*, don't it? Means they're looking for some thing they found once and it got away somehow, and now they got to *re*-search for it?" (57)

Miss Faust pleads that he take the elevator down and Knowles tells them the only direction they can go is down. When asked by Jonah if he knew the Hoenikker children, Knowles mumbles, "Babies full of rabies, yes, yes!" Jonah concludes that Knowles is insane. In Vonnegut's world, as in Mailer's, the balance between sanity and insanity is nearly always precarious. Many of his characters find themselves teetering on the edge of sanity and on the edge of organized society, struggling to avoid the one as much as the other.

Vonnegut has observed that he can create neither heroes nor villains. Felix Hoenikker is no more villian than Bokonon is a saint. Although Vonnegut's preferences are nearly always obvious, the quirks, habits, and idiosyncrasies of all his characters endear them to his readers, even when one finds their actions thoroughly at fault. Lyman Enders Knowles has a two-page part. Vonnegut could have dispensed with him as merely "a small ancient Negro" who operated the elevator during Jonah's tour of the Ilium works. But one of Vonnegut's standing concerns has been "what to do with people who have no use." Thus he does not dispense with Knowles or other bit-part characters. Each has the occasion to reveal a personality, and each seems to have some real function in the novel. Knowles is a spy in the House of Ilium. A smiling Greek among the topless towers, he warns others of the fall that is imminent.

While Jonah was in Ilium collecting data for his book about the A-Bomb, to be called *The Day the World Ended*, he saw a picture of Mona Ammons Monzano, the "sublime mongrel madonna" of San Lorenzo, in a special supplement to the *New York Sunday Times*. "On its cover was the profile of the most heartbreakingly beautiful girl I ever hope to see," Jonah says; "She was very young and very grave, too — and luminously compassionate and wise. She was as brown as chocolate, her hair was like golden flax" (72). One might guess that this blond-haired black girl is a modern day Helen; her photo woos Jonah from Ilium to the land of Bokonon.

Mona's father was a Finnish architect who arrived on San Lorenzo during the Second World War. He designed a hospital for the island, married a native woman named Celia, "fathered a perfect daughter and died" (103). Mona was adopted by "Papa" Monzano and as the years passed she unwillingly became the "national erotic symbol" of the island.

Jonah first lays eyes on Mona at the airport. He also observes a suggestive little scene during the arrival festivities. Mona has slipped off one of her sandals and with her bare foot "she was kneading and kneading and kneading — obscenely kneading — the instep of the flyer's boot" (123). Thus Jonah witnesses his first *boko-maru*, the sacred, secret ceremony of Bokononism that everybody practices but which is punishable by "the hook." One cannot help but smile at Vonnegut's humor here. Jonah and Mona must be meant for each other; their names fit together like two soles. Within a week they are engaged, and Jonah soon insists she *boko-maru* with no one else but him:

> Tears filled her eyes. She adored her promiscuity; was angered that I should try to make her feel shame. "I make people happy. Love is good, not bad."
> "As your husband, I'll want all your love for myself." She stared at me with widening eyes. "A *sin-wat!*"
> "What was that?"
> "A *sin-wat!*" she cried. "A man who wants all of somebody's love. That's very bad." (170)

Mona will not marry a *sin-wat*, she informs him, nor a man with no religion. Jonah concedes on all issues. He converts, learns that to Bokononists "it is very wrong not to love everyone exactly the same," and allows Mona to continue her indiscriminate *boko-marus* (170).

Their joy together is short-lived, however, for "Papa" Monzano accidentally touches off an ice-nine holocaust as he hastens his own painful death with a crystal of ice-nine. The crystal was given him by Franklin Hoenikker, who along with his brother and sister, acquired their ice-bombs at the time of their father's death. The *pool-pah* (or "shitstorm") that follows freezes all the waters of the earth and kills nearly all living things.

Among the few that survive the storms are Jonah and
Mona. They manage to climb down into an oubliette that
"Papa" had stocked for emergency survivial. Alone at last, in
the privacy of their own bomb shelter, Jonah looks at Mona
with thoughts of lust and possession. "Every greedy,
unreasonable dream I'd ever had about what a woman
should be came true in Mona." One can hardly be surprised
that, as the world froze to death about them, Mona refused
Jonah's advances.

> I will not go into the sordid sex episode that followed.
> Suffice it to say I was both repulsive and repulsed.
> The girl was not interested in reproduction — hated the
> idea. Before the tussle was over, I was given full credit by
> her, and by myself, too, for having invented the whole
> bizarre, grunting, sweating enterprise by which new human
> beings were made.... But then she said to me, gently, "It
> would be very sad to have a little baby now. Don't you
> agree?"
> "Yes," I agreed, murkily.
> "Well, that's the way little babies are made, in case you
> didn't know." (215)

How thoroughly in contrast Mona is with images of black
women in most white fiction. She is a far cry from the
"apocalyptic orgasm" in Mailer's fiction and the knowing
black women, technicians in their art, in Anderson's *Dark
Laughter*. She is embodiment of one of Vonnnegut's central
themes, "a purpose for human life...is to love whomever is
around to be loved."[72] The dimensions of Mona's character
slowly reveal themselves. Her *boko-maru* with the San
Lorenzan flyer is no more than an erotically "touching
moment." But the end of the world does not strike her as the
right time for sexual intercourse with Jonah. Soon afterward, seeing the multitude of her people on top of Mt.
McCabe, were they gathered to die together, she soon
touches ice-nine to her lips and joins them. Playful with
Jonah to the last minute, hoping to help him become a

Bokononist, and "still laughing a little, she touched her finger to the ground, straightened up, and touched her finger to her lips and dies," embracing death as easily as she lived life (221).

The crafty Bokonon does not join the thousands of islanders who have taken his advice. He told them that "God was surely trying to kill them, possibly because He was through with them, and that they should have the good manners to die" (220). Here is Bokonon's final illustration of how a perfectly good and humane religion can be founded on lies. At this point in the novel Bokonon is a voice for Vonnegut himself. As critic John Somer has expressed it, the problem Vonnegut has posed in all his novels is how to survive with dignity in an insane world.[73] *Cat's Cradle* presents a terribly bleak and absurd picture of the world. And Bokonon provides startling insight into the dilemma of survival, as well as some sound solutions. Both Vonnegut and his Bokonon outdo themselves in proving that they are outrageous fabricators. Like his author, Bokonon does not pretend to know the purpose of life, but he does devise artful, clever, and loving suggestions for living without the big answers.

Cat's Cradle is a novel about the end of the world, told by a narrator named Jonah who lives to write about it. He is a Jonah come back to life with Vonnegut's warning about the future of the planet. The Books of Bokonon begin with "All the true things I am about to tell you are shameless lies." To this Jonah adds, "Anyone unable to understand how a useful religion can be founded on lies will not understand this book either" (17). This last statement links artifice and lies to the pursuit of truth for Vonnegut, his narrator, and his black protagonist. Bokonon tells the San Lorenzans that God is finished with them and they should touch ice-nine to their lips and die with dignity: it is a compassionate lie.

It is easy to imagine that Vonnegut had recollections of Castro's Cuba, the missile crisis, and *Failsafe* in mind during his writing of *Cat's Cradle*. But the novel also resonates with the history of America's relationship with other nations and its frequent involvement in their internal politics.

It is also conceivable that Vonnegut was thinking of *The Emperor Jones* as he wrote the novel. The parallels and contrasts are certainly striking. Recall that Brutus Jones is obsessed with copying white values. He exploits the black islanders with the intention of amassing a fortune and escaping to Switzerland. Buried in O'Neill's play is the understanding that Jones fails because he dares to follow white values and because his race is unable to cleave itself from the "haunts and fears" of its tribal religion. Brutus is rendered a fool and a comic figure; Bokonon, by contrast, is both brilliant and a comedian. He fails to create a "par-a-dise" largely because of intervention by Americans bearing ice-nine. Bokonon and Vonnegut want to gently inoculate the reader with Bokononism and to warn him so that *Cat's Cradle* will not become a self-fulfilling prophecy.

Vonnegut manages so successfully with black character here because he cares about all his characters in a very individual and whimsical way. He creates neither heroes nor villains. Vonnegut's tone, throughout his novels, characteristically alternates between the serious and the comic. Thus his parodies (of religion and research, in this novel) are always prime vehicles for his ideas. Loving parody is for Vonnegut the foundation of understanding and respect. O'Neill describes Brutus Jones as "not altogether ridiculous." If anything is ridiculed here by Vonnegut the cultural primitivist, it is the false values of white America. In this context one cannot help but identify with Bokonon, who is "trying to survive in an insane world," as is everyone.

Vonnegut's Bokonon is one of the rare examples of a basically successful black portrait by a white writer. Bokonon's sophistication and complexity are themselves indicative of the care Vonnegut has taken in crafting his black portrait. That Bokonon is within the tradition of the black natural is unmistakable; he is the source of religious and moral values on San Lorenzo. He has created religious liturgy and writings simple enough to be understood by the uneducated islanders of San Lorenzo, yet containing dignity and universal human value. As Bokonon avoids condescension in his relationship with his people, so Vonnegut avoids either sarcasm or condescension in his relationship to Bokonon. Vonnegut does retain much of the distance and mystery that have been so characteristic of the natural mode, however. Bokonon is known through his writings and by oblique reference rather than through frequent or sustained direct contact. Not unlike Sam Fathers and Shago Martin, Bokonon appears and disappears; he is cloaked in mystery and shadow until the end of the novel. Vonnegut and the other writers of black naturals need to let go of the many devices that keep readers from more direct contact with black characters.

What is particularly rewarding about Vonnegut's black portrait is that Bokonon is not at the service of or even employed by white people. In fact, Bokonon is the first black natural encountered in this work who has independence from the white world. Several white Americans have been converted to Bokonon's religion, but he is not present to initiate them and, in fact, seems indifferent to their decision. Unlike most black naturals Bokonon lives in danger of death and hides among his people. He is a Caribbean Jesus, perhaps, yet he creates his religion not from divine inspiration but from practical necessity for the survival of his people. Although Bokonon does not become a public voice for his people, Vonnegut gives him an intellect as well as a sense of humor, thus producing one of the few white novels in which there is some sense of a black mind at work. Vonnegut upsets the apparent white assumption that blacks have bodies and soul but that they do not have the capacity for rational intelligence.

The case for Vonnegut's portrait of Bokonon is unexpectedly complicated by the television tape of *Between Time and Timbuktu*. Somehow, incredibly, between *Cat's Cradle* and this work Bokonon became white. He is also bearded and his dark blond hair is long and wavy. Before accusing Vonnegut of abandoning his black protagonist, one should observe that the book is based on a television script written by David O'Dell for a National Educational Television Playhouse production. Even though the film and the book that followed were studio-produced, Vonnegut bestowed his blessing on them in the "Preface" to the book. One can only speculate at this point on the reasons for a white Bokonon on film. Were the directors uneasy with a god like black figure before the screen? (That they were unable to find a suitable black actor seems implausible.)

Disturbed by the damage this sudden change of skin caused to Vonnegut's otherwise quite successful black portrait, I wrote him, expressing my astonishment. Vonnegut replied that he wished there were "an interesting story connected with this miscasting. But Bokonon became white, became the well-known actor Kevin McCarthy, simply because of the cheerful, slapdash, amateurism of educational television." Vonnegut admits that he was not consulted in the casting or the script until very near the end. It was, he confesses, his "Molly Bloom Period," during which he was "saying 'Yes' to everyone, no matter what he proposed." (The full letter is reprinted in note 74.)

Vonnegut justifies his carelessness "about what other people do with my work" by noting that nearly all his works are still in print and are part of the "public record." Be this as it may, one is left with the upsetting, perhaps unprecedented situation in which a black character becomes white in subsequent productions. An otherwise carefully drawn black character ultimately disappears, the apparent victim of neglect or prejudice.

*   *   *   *   *

Portraits of blacks as "naturals" have a number of common characteristics. Predominant among these similarities is the implied belief that blacks have something of value that whites have lost. Thus black naturals so often appear as entertainers, untaught teachers, fathers, and even priests. Black naturals entertain, educate, and lend assistance to white visitors. They are not only natural, but they are usually innocent, uncorrupted figures, whether living on the land or within the city. Their lives are both unspoiled and uncomplicated. There is an absence of change and conflict in their lives, a lack of growth, and a lack of tension. Black naturals just "are" — they function best in fable, myth, and legend. Because these blacks are so thoroughly a corrective tonic for white life, they are seldom portrayed as individuals with complex lives of their own. They seldom experience ambivalence or uncertainty, and seldom are they even tempted by corrupting influences.

Waldo Frank best expressed the implicit assumption within white portraits of black naturals. He observed, one recalls, that when blacks live in their "natural state" they draw from the sun and the soil "a grace which is refined . . . like the grace of a flower." Black naturals are connected to the soil and to animal life, even if they live in the city. Eudora Welty's Powerhouse is a walking jungle; he has a mouth like a monkey's and fingers like bananas. Aunt Phoenix talks to the animals as she walks through the Mississippi wilderness. Faulkner writes that "there was something running through Sam Father's veins which runs through the buck too."

Black naturals are more than just supremely at home in their environment — they are superhuman figures, perhaps best regarded as demi-gods. They clearly possess powers not available to ordinary mortals of either race. The words used to describe these figures are themselves indicative: "powerhouse," "un géant," "holy man," "father," "priest," "phoenix." If there is an essential scenario for tales of the "natural" it perhaps resembles this: a white male or female, greatly weakened by parentage, inheritance, and the cultural anemia of white civilization, encounters a black man or woman and receives a gift that is powerful and transforming. In Anderson's *Dark Laughter* Bruce Dudley learns how to laugh, relax, and have good sex, thanks to the "brown nigger girls" in New Orleans. e. e. cummings gazes "stupidly" and in awe at the "muscular miracle" of his friend Jean. Faulkner's Bayard Sartoris is pulled from his wrecked automobile by a "natural" man named John Henry. Dilsey nurtures the Compson children and represents moral value and spiritual grace. Ike McCaslin finds a father in Sam Fathers and is baptized into kinship with the mysteries of the great forest. Waldo Frank's *Virginia* seeks sexual fulfillment from the black man, John Cloud. Even Vonnegut's narrator, Jonah, receives a new religion and transforming world-view from the black holy man, Bokonon. Mailer's Stephen Rojack becomes a hero of the new world, initiated and empowered with magic by Shago Martin.

There is an ancillary dimension to this relationship of white initiate to black initiator that may be best described as a "search for lost fraternity." Occasionally the union of black and white involves the sexual fantasies of a white woman, but much more frequently one witnesses a fantasized relationship of black and white males. As previously mentioned, blacks often function as fraternal or paternal figures in Faulkner's fiction. John Henry cradles the injured white man's head in his lap as he drives Bayard to town. Bayard spends Christmas with a black family who offer him their loft and blankets and the next day share their meager Christmas meal with him. Sam Father's paternal and priestly relationship to Ike McCaslin hardly needs further mention. Even as Mailer's Stephen Rojack and Shago Martin battle each other, there is a complex interrelationship between the roles of lover and rival. e. e. cummings's friendship with Jean le Negre seems most accurately to express the phrase, "the image of memory and longing," which Irving Howe uses to characterize the tone of Faulkner's black portraits. That "beautiful pillar of black strutting muscle" with his "divine laugh" and the "whitest teeth on earth" became cummings's devoted friend. After the war he still remembers Jean and longs for their lost friendship. ("The flesh of your body is like the flesh of a very deep cigar. Which I am still and always quietly smoking.") The young white lady whose nostalgic poem caught Claude McKay's attention wrote, "All loose and free, O, lily me! / In muscled arms / of ebony." She continues, "I couldn't forget the black boy's eyes, / the black boy's shake, / the black boy's size." Obviously, not all of the images summarized here are implicitly sexual, but each does describe a relationship that creates, even if only briefly, the idealized union of black and white. In such experiences the white character leaves his or her own complex world to enter the world of the black natural.

As mentioned very early in this study, Freud expresses the great limitation in the primitivists' perspective by saying that the "attitude of primitivism" has always "failed to observe carefully." Primitivists have all too often "misunderstood what they saw" because they have already determined what they expected to find. And what they have wanted to find are better times or a better way of life somewhere else. All primitivism involves wish fulfillment and by consequence a sentimental disregard for the facts of primitive existence or for the persons being "primitivized."

Portraits of blacks as naturals, with their overly simplistic and often dehumanizing assumptions about black life, are not as overtly destructive as portraits in the savage mode, but they are corrosive nonetheless. Chief among their many defects is an assumption that blacks exist to serve whites; consequently they fail to accord to black characters the range of emotions characteristic of human behavior: anger as well as laughter; sexual indifference as well as eroticism; minds as well as bodies; thought as well as action. A further defect in such portraits is the assumption that social degradation is perfectly *natural* to these black characters, rather than imposed upon them by the racial oppression that has dominated the American social system. Thus, among the white writers discussed here neither cummings. Faulkner, nor Welty manages to create convincingly whole portraits of black life. Despite the shortcomings of their portraits, Mailer and Vonnegut have, by contrast, attempted to replace stereotyped naturals with more complex and lifelike black portraits.

Epilogue

Perhaps the most insidious and least understood form
of segregation is that of the word. And by this I mean
the word in all its complex formulations, from the
proverb to the novel and stage play, the word with all its
subtle power to suggest and foreshadow overt action
while magically disguising the moral consequences of
that action and providing it with symbolic and psychological justification. For if the word has the potency
to revive and make us free, it has also the power to
blind, imprison, and destroy.

The essence of the word is its ambivalence, and in
fiction it is never so effective and revealing as when
both potentials are operating simultaneously, as when it
mirrors both good and bad, as when it blows both hot
and cold in the same breath. Thus it is unfortunate for
the Negro that the most powerful formulations of
modern American fictional words have been so slanted
against him that when he approaches for a glimpse of
himself he discovers an image drained of humanity.
(Ralph Ellison, *Shadow and Act*)

As Ellison so powerfully writes, verbal segregation is an
insidious and dangerous form of literary slavery. White
writers, reflecting white tastes, seem to create their blacks to
satisfy various artistic, social, and political needs. But racial
stereotypes and images express personal beliefs just as
forcefully as social and political expediencies. In fact, one
approach to understanding the frequent presence of savage
and natural portraits is to see them as powerful expressions
of images emblazoned in the individual and racial unconscious. In Jungian terms, black naturals may be a projected
expression of the "wise old man" and savages an expression

179

of the evil or "shadow figure," both of which seem to reside within and consequentally may be projected onto others. These two modes of primitivism doubtlessly work out a variety of fantasies, dreams, and scenarios. Some of them probably reflect white racial theories and ingrained, subtly reinforced attitudes their authors were not consciously aware of. Such is the nature of the imagination, and of the words, in all their "complex formulations," that one uses to express it.

What generalizations about black people are implicit in the portraits discussed in this work? Writing within the savage mode almost always manages to reveal some further aspect of the black man's "true and savage nature." In the savage mode whites are confronted with either sexual assault or physical harm, although the violation is more often imagined than real. In most tales of the savage, even if the black man is vanquished, white characters receive the terror of "the black" they so thoroughly desire. As previously mentioned, there is for white characters a compulsion toward the "threatening blackness," as well as flight from the terror evoked.

An author writing in the natural mode usually portrays blacks who do not aspire much beyond their present circumstances. They are supremely at home in nature or on their local "turf." Unlike their savage cousins, they are embarrassingly kind to white folks. They hold the white boy's hand, mop his brow, suckle him at their breast, save him from fire and drowning, and rescue him from the wreckage of his civilization. They teach him about sex and life. And if he later forgets what he learned, they will patiently reeducate him. These black naturals, whether conjured up by Welty, Anderson, Faulkner, or Mailer, have surprising similarities in form and function. They are natural born exemplars of the life force, whether paternalistically (as with Sam Fathers) or sexually (as with Mailer's blacks). So long as whites continue to fear or covet what they believe blacks possess, white writers will continue to portray blacks as savages or naturals.

It is not at all surprising that Ellison, in looking at these and at other portraits of blacks in American writing, has declared that "these Negroes of fiction are counterfeits." His assessment is undeniable. White writers have been so busy creating black characters for symbolic and metaphoric purposes that they have often distorted them beyond recognizability. They serve as objective correlative either to a variety of white fears or to the aspirations of certain whites to escape from the "dying white soul" and regain contact with the life force. This distortion and dehumanizing simplification of character is often more dangerous in the natural than in the savage mode because it is so difficult to detect.

"Hideous wilderness" and "bountiful garden" are as pathetically inadequate images of landscape as "savage" and "natural" are of a human race. To some degree, the writing of Crane, Welty, cummings, Frank, Mailer, and Vonnegut calls into question popular white images of black character. In each of these works the author intends to place himself somewhere between the simplistic white conception of "blackness" and the black character himself. Through ironic revelations these writers attempt to achieve realistic or at least more accurate portraits of blacks. While being appreciative for their more sensitive attempts at black portraiture, readers of these works may nonetheless become painfully aware of the limitations of even these portraits. By way of example, two of the characters portrayed by this group of writers are brain-damaged (Henry Johnson and Little Lee Roy) and most of the others are so detached and laconic that they seem separated from the reader by an invisible wall. Among the works and characters considered, only Welty's Powerhouse, Frank's John Cloud, Mailer's Shago Martin, and Vonnegut's Bokonon move significantly beyond stereotype to suggest a reality and presence of their own.

Why is it, one might well ask, that white writers function so inadequately when confronting blacks? Some of the reasons are fairly obvious. For one, they have seldom really looked at blacks as individuals, asking the kinds of penetrating questions they would ask about white characters. For another, white writers have been more interested in blacks as symbols or mirrors than as human entities. Beyond this, there are the very real barriers between the races that are responsible for much of the distance and uncertainty, and there are all the special little traps that these two modes of primitivism hold open to white writers. Consequently, "well-intentioned" whites seldom succeed in establishing recognizable and richly ambivalent black portraits, even if they have succeeded in denying the sufficiency of primitivism as a means of delineating character.

To some degree those white writers who have had closer contact with black life have fared better than the others. Waldo Frank, one recalls, traveled through the South with the black writer, Jean Toomer. e. e. cummings had the "good fortune" of a prison term in the "Enormous Room" with a black man named Jean. By contrast, Crane's source for his "monster" was the childhood image of a deformed black man who shoveled coal. O'Neill and Lindsay whetted their imaginations on the most superficial of sources: recalled images of local "colored folks," the tales of Edgar Allan Poe, and Stanley's *In Darkest Africa*. Of Vonnegut it might be said that he cares about all people and thus pays careful attention to even his minor characters. His endless appetite for irony also facilitates the reversals in white and black roles he establishes in *Cat's Cradle*. Although one cannot speculate on the degree of Mailer's firsthand contact with black life, it is obvious that he has a Nietzschean regard for blacks as "supermen." There are great limitations to Mailer's unitary vision of black life, but despite these he creates in Shago Martin a character who survives his author's typecasting to emerge as a vivid and memorable portrait.

But these do not seem sufficient explanations for the inadequacies in portraiture discussed here. It is not unjust to expect a greater sensitivity and a more abundant and sympathetic imagination from writers than from the general public. As Vonnegut himself has said, a writer is supposed to be a "specialized cell," a "canary in the coal mine," who is more sensitive to the human condition than are the other cells of the organism.[1] The burden is on writers to bridge the barriers, distances, and stereotypes through contact with "The other" and through the liberating power of the imagination. When this happens, as William Gass expresses it, "Fiction's fruit survives its handling and continues growing off the tree. A great character has an endless interest; its fascination never wanes."[2]

No writer has dramatized the ascription of primitivism to blacks by whites more powerfully than the black writer Imamu Baraka (formerly LeRoi Jones) in his play, *Dutchman*.[3] The play is remarkably pertinent here because it moves skillfully through the field of problems under discussion and establishes the individualities of both its black and its white protagonists. Baraka's male lead, Clay Williams, is a young, black, college graduate who wears a dark, three-button suit and lives in suburban New Jersey. While riding a Manhattan subway, he is seductively approached by a sleazy white woman named Lula, who tells him she has come searching him out.

Clay is at first attracted by Lula's suggestiveness. He later begins to recoil from her advances when she tells him how to invite her to a Harlem party in a way that will excite her imagination. She literally puts words in the black man's mouth and then angers when he strays from her scenario. Lula sketches out their evening; after the party they will go to her apartment and "talk about your manhood." She tells Clay she will "make a map of it."

Lula believes that beneath the three-button suit and middle-class image lies a sexual savage, a funky black man

who is throbbing with desire for her. She calls out, "Come on
Clay. Let's do the nasty. Rub bellies. Rub bellies." The
limitations to her conception of black people are unmistakable. She expects the black man to submit to her sexual
whimsey, to be as moldable as a lump of clay. By implication,
all blacks are to submit to the poking and shaping of white
culture or their fate will be the same as Clay's. As she
conducts her sexual assault on Clay, Lula is not unlike all
racists and exploiters. She admits, "I lie a lot. It helps me
control the world." This should have been sufficient warning
to Clay not to eat the apple she offers, but he does and is soon
hopelessly lost, a black man "in dutch." Understanding the
title another way, Lula is the Dutchman, engaged in a
contemporary form of slave trade. As in the past, a slave
either submits and lives or rebels and dies. Lula pleads with
him once more to "do the gritty grind, like your ol'
rag-head mammy" (31). Again he refuses, trying to avoid a
scene in the subway. She yells at him, "You middle-class
black bastard . . . .You liver-lipped white man. You would-be
Christian. You ain't no nigger, you're just a dirty white
man" (31).

Trying to preserve his "cool" throughout her diatribe,
Clay finally reaches a saturation point. He removes the mask
he has chosen to wear and lashes out at Lula and all whites
who would primitivize or otherwise categorize black people.
Venting a hatred and loathing of all white people that he
usually suppresses behind the mask, Clay gains in stature
and integrity with each succeeding line:

> Let me be who I feel like being. Uncle Tom. Thomas.
> Whoever. It's none of your business. You don't know
> anything except what's there for you to see. An act. Lies.
> Device. Not the pure heart, the pumping black heart. You
> don't ever know that. And I sit here, in this buttoned-up
> suit, to keep myself from cutting out all your throats. I
> mean wantonly. You great liberated whore! You fuck

some black man, and right away you're an expert on black people. What a lotta shit that is (34).

With the words of Clay's song still ringing in her ears, Lula stabs him to death and, with the help of the subway "audience," throws his body onto the tracks.

In her book *Black Masks*, Nancy Tischler comments, "Clearly the modern tendency is to see the Negro not as a natural anything, but as a blank tablet and a product of environment."[4] There is, however, considerable evidence to the contrary. Ellison's "Sybil" and Baraka's "Lula" certainly do not corroborate this thesis.

The writers discussed in this study are all accomplished artists, some of them regarded as among America's finest writers. Yet nearly all these writers fail in some important way to establish the necessary complexity and "selfhood" of their black characters. Like Scylla and Charybdis, the dual images of savage and natural yawn invitingly and deceptively before the white writer. Unexamined acceptance of either stereotype is a facile solution to the difficulty faced by a white writer in attempting to describe black lives. As Charles Mayer has expressed this dilemma, blacks have had to overcome stereotypes and other barriers in creating a sense of selfhood and "the white man's converse problem (has been) recognizing that selfhood and responding with understanding and compassion."[5]

At its worst, literary primitivism is a servitude of black fictional characters to their white authors' needs or preconceptions. This is a bondage that impedes the vital process of the sympathetic imagination. It is probably not unjust to accuse most of the writers considered here of a failure of vision. It is a failure in perception and in rendering black characters in complex, compassionate and lifelike ways.

Although it is doubtful that white fascination with primitivism and black character will soon diminish, one can hope that future white writers will be better prepared to detect and penetrate these and other stereotypes of blacks, and of other special groups of people. The history of cultural primitivism suggests that the further society withdraws from nature, the more complex and pervasive is its longing for at least vestiges of primitive life and for works of the imagination in which the longing finds fulfillment.

The lack of complexity that has characterized the "primitives" examined here has always been more an illusion held by civilized man than a fact of primitive life. The white writer as primitivist simplifies and stylizes life in nature not so much to understand "primitive character" as to rationalize and presumably to clarify his own experience, to justify his racial attitudes, or to supplement his cultural needs. In assessing many of the same works, Ralph Ellison has observed that, taken collectively, they seemed to him like a huge drama being "acted out upon the body of a Negro giant, who, lying trussed up like Gulliver, forms the stage and the scene upon which and within which the action unfolds."[6]

These limitations in sensibility regarding blacks are particularly regrettable because they hinder white readers in their attempts to visualize black life and experience. Like all stereotyping, they allow reader and writer to substitute easily accepted masks and conventions for critical thought and honest excursions of the imagination. They furnish strategies whereby both reader and writer may avoid grappling with the inevitable variety, complexity, and ambiguity of human nature.

Notes

All sources of direct value or influential to this study receive mention here and within the text. The Schomberg Collection of The New York Public Library and the Beineke Library, Yale University, were particularly helpful sources, as was the library of the University of Massachusetts, at Amherst.

Preface

1. Ralph Ellison. *Invisible Man* (New York: Random House, 1947). pp. 311-312.
2. Langston Hughes. *The Big Sea* (New York: Alfred A. Knopf, 1910). P. 325.
3. Ibid.
4. Although this is not a study of black literature, some black writers do use forms of primitivism, most often to purposes quite different from those of white writers.
5. Frederick Hoffman, *The Twenties: American Writing in the Postwar Decade* (New York: The Viking Press, 1949), p. 269.
6. Robert Bone, *The Negro Novel in America* (New Haven, Conn.: Yale University Press, 1965), p. 60.
7. For a full definition of "savagism" see Roy Harvey Pearce, *The Savages of America: A Study of the Indian and the Idea of Civilization* (Baltimore, Md.: Johns Hopkins University Press, 1965).
8. For a detailed study of white stereotypes of black character, see Sterling Brown's classic work, *The Negro in American Fiction* (Washington, D.C.: Association for Negro Folk Education, 1937).
9. William Gass, *Fiction and the Figures of Life* (New York: Vintage Books, 1959), p. 35.

Chapter 1. Background and Prototypes

1. For a thorough exploration of the complex pastoral, see Leo Marx, *The Machine in the Garden: Technology and the Pastoral Ideal in America* (New York: Oxford University Press, 1967). Special acknowledgment is due Marx for his discussion of the conflicting views of the nature of nature held in the Old World and the New at the time of settlement.
2. William Strachey, "A true reportory of the wracke, and redemption of Sir Thomas Gates Knight; upon, and from the Ilands of the Bermudas...," *Hakluytus Posthumus, or Purchas His Pilgrimes*. ed. Samuel Purchas (Glasgow: MacLehose, 1906), 19:6.

3. *Bradford's History of Plymouth Plantation, 1606-1646,* ed. William T. Davis (New York: C. Scribner's Sons, 1908), pp. 94-96.

4. Arthur Barlowe, "The first voyage made to the coasts of America..." in Richard Hakluyt, *The Principal Navigations, Voyages, Traffiques and Discoveries of the English Nation* (Glasgow: J. MacLehose and Sons, 1904), 8:298.

5. Leslie Fiedler, *Waiting for the End* (New York: Stein and Day, 1965), p. 113.

6. Henry David Thoreau, *A Week on the Concord and Merrimack Rivers* (New York: Holt, Rinehart & Winston, 1963), p. 272.

7. Ibid., p. 274.

8. Ibid.

9. Ibid., p. 232.

10. Ibid.

11. Kenneth Clark, *The Gothic Revival* (New York: Humanities Press, 1970).

12. Bertrand Evans, *Gothic Drama from Walpole to Shelley* (Berkeley, Calif.: University of California Press, 1947), p. 9.

13. Leslie Fiedler, *Love and Death in the American Novel* (New York: Stein and Day, 1967), p. 140.

14. Ibid.

15. Ibid., p. 142.

16. Charles Brockden Brown, *Edgar Huntly, or Memoirs of a Sleep-Walker* (Port Washington, N.Y.: AMS Press, 1963), pp. 4, 28.

17. Fiedler, *Love and Death,* p. 155.

18. Roy Harvey Pearce, *The Savages of America: A Study of the Indian and the Idea of Civilization* (Baltimore, Md.: Johns Hopkins University Press, 1965), p. 20.

19. Cotton Mather, *The Negro Christianized* (Boston, 1706), p. 5.

20. John Saffin, "The Negro's Character," in George Moore, *Notes on the History of Slavery in Massachusetts* (New York, 1866), p. 256. With this poem Saffin was attempting to shout down Samuel Sewall's rare plea, in his *The Selling of Joseph* (1700), to free the blacks.

21. Milton Cantor, "The Image of the Negro in Colonial Literature," *Images of the Negro in American Literature,* ed. Seymour L. Gross and John Edward Hardy (Chicago: University of Chicago Press, 1966), p. 34.

22. For a full discussion of these works see Sidney Kaplan, "Introduction," *The Narrative of Arthur Gordon Pym* (New York: Hill and Wang, 1960), and Kaplan's "Herman Melville and the American National Sin: The Meaning of *Benito Cereno,*" *Journal of Negro History* 41 (1956): 311-38; 17 (1957): 11-37.

23. Joel Chandler Harris, *Free Joe and Other Georgian Sketches* (New York: P.F. Collier, 1887), p. 4.

24. Sigmund Freud, *Civilization and Its Discontents,* trans. James Strachey (New York: W.W. Norton & Co., 1961), pp. 29.

25. Ibid., p. 30.

26. Ibid., p. 66.

27. Arthur Lovejoy, Foreword to *Primitivism and the Idea of Progress in English Popular Literature of the Nineteenth Century* by Lois Whitney (Baltimore, Md.: Johns Hopkins University Press, 1935), p. vi.

28. Ibid., p. xi.

29. Ibid., p. xv.

30. Robert Beverley, *History and Present State of Virginia*, ed. Louis B. Wright (Chapel Hill, N.C.: University of North Carolina Press, 1947), pp. 17.

31. Ibid., p. 156.

32. *Complete Works of Edgar Allan Poe*, ed. James A. Harrison (New York: G. D. Sproul, 1902), 1:271.

33. Even Harriet Beecher Stowe, despite her fervent desire to see slavery abolished, extolled the virtues of such benevolent slave owners as the Shelbys and spoke of blacks, generally, as home-loving, sensitive, docile, and loyal to their masters.

34. For a general discussion of "the contented slave" convention, see Sterling Brown, *The Negro in American Fiction* (Washington, D.C., 1937).

35. Irwin Russell, "Christmas Night in the Quarters," *Collected Poems* (New York: Century, 1888). While squarely within the plantation tradition, Russell adds a dimension characteristic of the natural mode. He finds in black life certain positive values that he believes his culture could well emulate: spontaneity, unrestrained expression of feelings, exuberance and inventiveness in song and dance. In general, postbellum writers are chronological primitivists who desire to restore the South to its antebellum state.

36. V. F. Calverton, *The Liberation of American Literature* (New York: Charles Scribners Sons, 1932), pp. 147-148.

Chapter 2. The Savages

1. Sterling Brown, "Negro Character as Seen by White Authors," *Journal of Negro Education* 2 (April 1933); 191.

2. Roy Harvey Pearce, *The Savages of America: A Study of the Indian and the Idea of Civilization* (Baltimore, Md.: Johns Hopkins University Press, 1965), p. 243.

3. The *Century* rejected the story in 1897 and considered it "simply a horrible thing." Harold Frederic, the novelist, urged Crane to throw it away, but "Howells considered it the greatest short story ever written by an American." See Robert Stallman, *Stephen Crane* (New York: Braziller, 1968), p. 332.

4. Donald Gibson, *The Fiction of Stephen Crane* (Carbondale, Ill.: Southern Illinois University Press, 1968), p. 136.

5. Ibid., p. 137.

6. Charles Mayer, "Social Forms vs Human Brotherhood in Crane's *The Monster,"Ball state University Forum* 14 (Summer 1973): 33.

7. Gibson, *Fiction of Stephen Crane*, p. 136.

8. Stephen Crane, *The Complete Short Stories and Sketches of Stephen Crane*, ed. Thomas Gullason (Garden City, N.Y., Doubleday 1963), p. 431. Subsequent page references to this source will be indicated within the text.

9. Stallman, *Stephen Crane*, p. 333.

10. This is not unlike the sentiment ironically expressed in Blake's "The Little Black Boy," who says of the English child, "white as an angel," "I'll shade him from the heat...And then I'll stand and stroke his silver hair,/ And he will then love me." In "The Monster" that love is accorded the black figure only after his "death" while saving the white child from the heat of his father's burning garden.

11. Sy Kahn, "Stephen Crane and the Giant Voices in the Night: An Explication of 'The Monster,' " *Essays in Modern American Literature*, ed. Richard Langford (De Land, Fla.: Everett-Edwards, 1963), pp. 36-37.

12. Stallman, *Stephen Crane*, p. 344.

13. Ibid.

14. Ralph Ellison, *Shadow and Act* (New York: Random House, 1953), pp. 87-88.

15. Thomas Beer, *Stephen Crane: A Study in American Letters* (Garden City, N.Y.: A.A. Knopf, 1923), p. 164.

16. See Thomas A. Gullason, "The Symbolic Unity of *The Monster*," *Modern Language Notes* 75 (1960): 663.

17. Stallman, *Stephen Crane*, p. 344.

18. Eleanor Ruggles, *The West-Going Heart: A Life of Vachel Lindsay* (New York: W.W. Norton, Inc., 1959), pp. 205-6. Subsequent page references to this source will appear within the text.

19. Raymond Perkey, *Vachel Lindsay: 1879-1931* (Paris: Nizet, 1968), p. 100.

20. Apparently Lindsay and his biographer imagined that this response by the Negro waiters justified the poem, or perhaps verified its authenticity.

21. Travis Bogard, *Contour in Time: The Plays of Eugene O'Neill* (New York: Oxford University Press, 1972), p. 134.

22. Croswell Bowen, *The Curse of the Misbegotten: A Tale of the House of O'Neill* (New York: McGraw-Hill Book Co., 1959), p. 132.

23. *New York Tribune*, 4 November 1920.

24. Bogard, *Contour in Time*, p. 134.

25. Doris Abramson, *Negro Playwrights in the American Theatre, 1925-1959* (New York: Columbia University Press, 1969), p. 27.

26. Bogard, *Contour in Time*, p. 134.

27. Robert Bone, *The Negro Novel in America* (New Haven, Conn.: Yale University Press, 1965), p. 60.

28. Ibid.

29. Alain Locke, *The New Negro* (New York: Boni and Liveright, 1925), p. 5.

30. Bogard, *Contour in Time*, p. 135.

31. Ibid.

32. Bowen, *Curse of the Misbegotten*, p. 132.

33. Ibid., p. 131.

34. Arthur and Barbara Gelb, *O'Neill* (New York: Harper & Row, 1960), p. 449.

35. Eugene O'Neill, *The Emperor Jones* (New York: Appleton, 1921), pp. 10-11. Subsequent page references to this edition will appear within the text.

36. Eugene Waith, "Eugene O'Neill: An Exercise in Unmasking," in *O'Neill*, ed. John Gassner (Englewood Cliffs, N.J.: Prentice-Hall, 1964), p. 33.

37. John Gassner, "The Nature of O'Neill's Achievement: A Summary and Appraisal," in *O'Neill*, ed. Gassner, p. 166.

38. Edwin Engle, *The Haunted Heroes of Eugene O'Neill* (Cambridge, Mass: Harvard University Press, 1953), p. 54.

39. Ibid.

40. In this context of established white stereotypes of black people, Emil Roy's comment (see *Comparative Drama* 2 [Spring 1968]: 22ff.) that "Jones's red pants and

gaudy throne link him with suffering heroes like Prometheus," and "disguised gods like Apollo" is wide of the mark.

41. Langston Hughes, *The Big Sea* (New York: Alfred A. Knopf, 1940), pp. 258-59.

42. Benjamin Brawley, "The Negro in American Fiction," *Dial* 60 (1916): 445.

43. For detailed discussion of this topic, see Seymour L. Gross, "Stereotype to Archetype: The Negro in American Literary Criticism," in *Images of the Negro in American Literature,* ed. Seymour Gross and John Edward Hardy (Chicago: University of Chicago Press, 1966), pp. 1-26.

44. George Morse, "The Fictitious Negro," *Outlook and Independent* 152 (1929): 678-79.

45. Bogard, *Contour in Time,* p. xiii.

46. Paul Carter, *Waldo Frank* (New York: Twayne Publishers, 1967), pp. 54-55.

47. *Memoirs of Waldo Frank,* ed. Alan Trachtenberg (Amherst, Mass.: University of Massachusetts Press, 1973), p. 104.

48. Ibid., p. 105.

49. Ibid., p. 55.

50. Waldo Frank, *Our America* (New York: Boni and Liveright, 1919).

51. Carter, *Waldo Frank,* pp. 231-32.

52. Ibid., pp. 33, 37.

53. Waldo Frank, *In The American Jungle* (New York: Farrar and Rinehart, 1936).

54. Waldo Frank, *Holiday* (New York: Boni and Liveright, 1923), p. 125. Subsequent page references to this source will appear in the text.

55. Claude McKay, *A Long Way from Home* (New York: L. Furman, 1937), p. 346.

56. Virginia's description of the black community is similar to Lindsay's picture of a "Congo paradise" at the time of its conversion. Music fills the air and to Virginia the cabins look like painted toys. For Lindsay, the apostles fill the air with their heavenly cry; the new "Negro Nation" is a land safe for "babes at play." The difference lies in Frank's sensitivity to the realities of black life, a quality of understanding that apparently did not occur to or interest Lindsay.

57. There are several surprising parallels between this scene and the conclusion of Imamu Baraka's *Dutchman.* In both, a black man is destroyed for refusing to play the sexual role demanded of him by a white woman.

58. Carter, *Waldo Frank,* pp. 55-56.

59. Darwin Turner, *In A Minor Chord* (Carbondale, Ill.: Southern Illinois University Press, 1971).

60. Nancy Tischler, *Black Masks: Negro Characters in Modern Southern Fiction,* (University Park, Pa.: Pennsylvania State University Press, 1969), p. 60.

61. Tennessee Williams, *Sweet Bird of Youth* (New York: New Directions, 1959), pp. 79-80, 97.

62. John Henrick Clarke, ed., William Styron's Nat Turner: Ten Black Writers Respond, (Boston: Beacon Press, 1968).

Chapter 3. The Naturals

1. Irwin Russell, "Christmas Night in the Quarters," *Collected Poems* (New York: Century, 1888).

2. e.e. cummings, *The Enormous Room* (New York: Modern Library, 1934), p. 270.

Subsequent page references to this source will appear within the text.

3. For more detailed discussion see Charles Nilon, *Faulkner and the Negro* (New York: Citadel, 1965), and Irving Howe, *William Faulkner: A Critical Study* (New York: Random House, 1951).

4. Cleanth Brooks, *William Fualkner: The Yoknapatawpha Country* (New Haven, Conn.: Yale University Press, 1963), p. 44.

5. Frederick L. Gwynn and Joseph L. Blotner, *Faulkner in the University*, (Charlottesville, Va.: University of Virginia Press, 1959), p. 68.

6. Brooks, *William Faulkner*, p. 45.

7. Edmund Volpe, *A Reader's Guide to William Faulkner* (New York: Farrar, Straus & Giroux, 1964), p. 27.

8. William Faulkner, *Go Down, Moses* (New York: Random House, 1942), p. 167.

9. *William Faulkner: A Critical Study* (New York: Random House, 1952), pp. 134, 117.

10. William Faulkner, *Sartoris* (New York: Harcourt, Brace, 1929), p. 339. Subsequent page references to this work will appear within the text.

11. Brooks, *William Faulkner*, p. 113.

12. Howe, *Faulkner*, p. 41.

13. Volpe, *Reader's Guide*, p. 71.

14. Ibid., p. 72.

15. Isaac McCaslin's first trip to the Big Bottom is described similarly in "The Bear."

16. He does so in the fashion of Blake's "The Little Black Boy," who will shade the "little English boy" from the heat and "stroke his silver hair."

17. Howe, *Faulkner*, p. 40.

18. Ibid., p. 123.

19. Gwynn and Blotner, eds., *Faulkner in the University*, p. 85.

20. William Faulkner, *The Sound and the Fury* (New York: Random House, 1929), p. 281. Subsequent page references to this work will appear within the text.

21. Lawrence Thompson, "Mirror Analogues in *The Sound and the Fury*," in *Faulkner: A Collection of Critical Essays*, ed. Robert Penn Warren (Englewood Cliffs, N.J.: Prentice-Hall, 1966).

22. David Williams, *Faulkner's Women* (Montreal: McGill-Queen's University Press, 1977), p. 93.

23. Howe, *Faulkner*, p. 123.

24. Gwynn and Blotner, eds., *Faulkner in the University*, p. 5.

25. Faulkner, *Go Down, Moses*, p. 166. Subsequent page references to this source will appear in the text.

26. William Van O'Connor, "The Wilderness Theme in Faulkner's 'The Bear,' " *Accent* 22 (Winter 1953): 20.

27. Melvin Blackman, *Faulkner: The Major Years* (Bloomington, Ind.: Indiana University Press, 1966), p. 164.

28. Volpe, *Reader's Guide*, p. 201.

29. Otis B. Wheeler, "Faulkner's Wilderness," *American Literature* 36 (January 1965): 167.

30. Gwynn and Blotner, eds., *Faulkner at the University*, pp. 245-46.

31. For a discussion of this particular point, see Marvin Klotz, "Procrustian Revision in Faulkner's *Go Down, Moses,"American Literature* 36 (March 1965): 1-16.

32. Louise Gossett, *Violence in Recent Southern Fiction* (Durham, N. C.: Duke University Press, 1965), p. 106.

33. Eudora Welty, "Pageant of Birds," *New Republic* 25 (October 1943): 565-67.

34. Eudora Welty, "Ida M'Toy," *Accent* 2 (Summer 1942): 214-22.

35. Eudora Welty, "Where is the Voice Coming From?" *New Yorker* (6 July 1963): 24-25.

36. Eudora Welty, "Keela, the Outcast Indian Maiden," *Selected Stories of Eudora Welty* (New York: Modern Library, 1936), p. 80. Subsequent page references to this work will appear in the text.

37. Robert Van Gelder, "An Interview with Eudora Welty," in *Writers and Writing* (New York: Saunders, 1946), p. 190.

38. Alfred Appel, Jr., *A Season of Dreams: The Fiction of Eudora Welty* (Baton Rouge, La.: Louisiana State University Press, 1965), p. 166.

39. William Jones, "Welty's 'A Worn Path,' " *Explicator* 15 (June 1957): Item 57.

40. Neil Isaacs, "Life for Phoenix," *Sewanee Review* 71 (1963): 75-81.

41. John Edward Hardy, "Eudora Welty's Negroes," *Images of the Negro in American Literature,* ed. Seymour L. Gross and John Edward Hardy (Chicago: University of Chicago Press, 1966), p. 226.

42. Appel, *Season of Dreams,* p. 170.

43. Hardy, "Eudora Welty's Negroes," p. 226.

44. Ibid., p. 229.

45. Appel, *Season of Dreams,* p. 48.

46. Ibid., p. 149.

47. Gossett, *Violence in Recent Southern Fiction,* p. 110.

48. Appel, *Season of Dreams,* p. 103.

49. Ralph Ellison, *Shadow and Act* (New York: Random House, 1953), p. 47.

50. Norman Mailer, "The White Negro" (San Francisco, Calif.: City Lights Books, 1958).

51. Norman Mailer, *Advertisements for Myself* (New York: G.P. Putnam's Sons, 1959), p. 17.

52. Ibid., p. 333.

53. Barry Leeds, *The Structured Vision of Norman Mailer* (New York: New York University Press, 1969), p. 227.

54. Mailer, "The White Negro," p. 11.

55. Ibid.

56. James Baldwin, *Nobody Knows My Name* (New York: Dial Press, 1961), p. 184.

57. Ibid., pp. 173, 174.

58. Eldridge Cleaver, *Soul on Ice* (New York: McGraw-Hill, 1968), p. 108.

59. Ibid., p. 105.

60. Ironically, critic Robert Bone has accused Baldwin of implying in his fiction that "the holy and liberating orgasm" comes only from violating sexual taboos through biracial and homosexual relationships.

61. Norman Mailer, *An American Dream* (New York: Dial Press, 1965), p. 179. Subsequent page references to this source will appear within the text.

62.	Robert Solataroff, *Down Mailer's Way* (Urbana, Ill.: University of Illinois Press, 1974), p. 133.

63.	See Sir James George Frazer, *The New Golden Bough* (Garden City, N.Y.: Doubleday & Co., 1961), and Mircea Eliade, *The Sacred and the Profane* (New York: Harcourt Brace Jovanovich, 1959).

64.	Tony Tanner, *City of Words* (London: Jonathan Cape, 1971), p. 360.

65.	Ibid., p. 363.

66.	Ibid., p. 355.

67.	Mailer, *Dream,* p. 194.

68.	Joyce Carol Oates, "Out of the Machine," in *Will the Real Norman Mailer Please Stand Up?* ed. Laura Adams (Port Washington, N.Y.: Kennikat Press, 1974), p. 216.

69.	Kurt Vonnegut, Jr., *Cat's Cradle* (New York: Delacort Press, 1965). Subsequent page references to this source will appear within the text.

70.	Kurt Vonnegut, Jr., *Between Time and Timbuktu* (New York: Delacort Press, 1972).

71.	Ibid., p. 89.

72.	Kurt Vonnegut, Jr., *Sirens of Titan* (New York: Dell Publishing Co., 1959), p. 313.

73.	See John Somer, "Geodesic Vonnegut; Or, If Buckminster Fuller Wrote Novels," in *The Vonnegut Statement,* ed. Jerome Klinkowitz and John Somer (New York: Delacorte Press, 1973), pp. 221-54.

74.	The complete text of the letter from Kurt Vonnegut follows:

228 East 48th Street, NYC 10017
June 28, 1975

Professor John R. Cooley
Department of English
Western Michigan
Kalamazoo, Michigan 49001

Dear Professor Cooley:—

I will tell you something even screwier than Bokonon's being white in the TV show: You are the only person who has ever asked me about it, even though the part was so terribly weakened by his being, as you say, whitewashed. What mattered even more to me was that Bokonon be a *Caribbean* black. Oh well, what the hell.

I wish there were an interesting story connected with this miscasting. But Bokonon became white, became the well-known actor Kevin McCarthy, simply because of the cheerful, slapdash, amateurism of educational television. A lot of actors had to be hired in a hurry. Kevin was willing and famous and likeable, and had been in another work of mine, so he got the job.

I wasn't consulted on the casting, or on the script, either, until very late in the game. I gave permission for the TV people to do what they pleased with my stuff. I was busy on other projects. I *did* come in near the end, and did do some desperate and fast writing, to try to make the show more intelligible. But many things did not work, including Bokonon's being white. But the budget was exhausted. We had no

money with which to patch up even the really awful parts. So that was that. Hi ho.
What makes me so careless about what other people do with my work is that almost all my books and stories remain in print. Proof of what I really said, as opposed to what someone else says I said, is easy to come by. I have no dead books which are now represented only by somebody else's films.

You say that you have been puzzled, and perhaps a little upset, by the miscasting. So I apologize. I am ultimately to blame. It all happened during a crazy period in my life, which I now call my "Molly Bloom Period," during which I was saying "Yes" to everyone, no matter what he proposed. That is now behind me.

Cheers-

Kurt Vonnegut, Jr.

Epilogue

1. Robert Scholes, "A Talk with Kurt Vonnegut, Jr.," in *The Vonnegut Statement,* ed. Jerome Klinkowitz and John Somer (Boston: Delacorte Press, 1973).

2. William Gass, *Fiction and the Figures of Life* (New York: Vintage Books, 1959), p. 35.

3. Imamu Baraka, *Dutchman* (New York: William Morrow & Co., 1964). Subsequent page references to this work will appear within the text.

4. Nancy Tischler, *Black Masks: Negro Characters in Modern Southern Fiction* (University Park, Pa.: Pennsylvania State University Press, 1969), p. 195.

5. Charles Mayer, "Social Forms vs. Human Brotherhood in Crane's *The Monster,"Ball State University Forum* 14 (Summer 1973): 29.

6. Ralph Ellison, *Shadow and Act* (New York: Random House, 1953), p. 46.

Selected Bibliography

Abramson, Doris. *Negro Playwrights in the American Theatre, 1925-1959.* New York: Columbia University Press, 1969.

Appel, Alfred, Jr. *A Season of Dreams: The Fiction of Eudora Welty.* Baton Rouge, La.: Louisiana State University Press, 1965.

Backman, Melvin. *Faulkner: The Major Years.* Bloomington, Ind.: Indiana University Press, 1966.

Baldwin, James. *Nobody Knows My Name.* New York: Dial Press, 1961.

Barlowe, Captain Arthur. "The first voyage made to the coasts of America ..." In Richard Hakluyt, *The Principal Navigations, Voyages, Traffiques and Discoveries of the English Nation.* Glasgow: J. MacLehose and Sons, 1904.

Beer, Thomas. *Stephen Crane: A Study in American Letters.* Garden City, N.Y.: A.A. Knopf, 1923.

Bennett, Lerone, Jr. *Before the Mayflower: A History of the Negro in America, 1619-1962.* Chicago: Johnson Publishing Co., 1962.

Beverley, Robert. *The History and Present State of Virginia.* Edited by Louis B. Wright. Chapel Hill, N.C.: University of North Carolina Press, 1947.

Bogard, Travis. *Contour in Time: The Plays of Eugene O'Neill.* New York: Oxford University Press, 1972.

Bone, Robert. *The Negro Novel in America.* New Haven, Conn.: Yale University Press, 1965.

Bowen, Corswell. *The Curse of the Misbegotten: A Tale of the House of O'Neill.* New York: McGraw-Hill Book Co., 1959.

Bradford, Roark. *John Henry.* New York: Literary Guild, 1931.

Bradford, William. *History of Plymouth Plantation, 1606-1646*. Edited by William T. Davis. New York: C. Scribner's Sons, 1908.

Brawley, Benjamin. *A Social History of the American Negro*. New York: Macmillan Co., 1921.

Brooks, Cleanth. *William Faulkner: The Yoknapatawpha Country*. New Haven, Conn.: Yale University Press, 1963.

Brown, Charles Brockden. *Edgar Huntley, or Memoirs of a Sleep-Walker*. Port Washington, N.Y.: AMS Press, 1963.

Brown, Sterling A. *The Negro in American Fiction*. Washington, D.C.: Association for Negro Folk Education, 1937.

————. "Negro Character as Seen by White Authors." *Journal of Negro Education* 2 (April 1933): 179-203.

Calverton, V. F. *The Liberation of American Literature*. New York: Charles Scribner's, 1932.

Cantor, Milton. "The Image of the Negro in Colonial Literature." In *Images of the Negro in American Literature*, edited by Seymour L. Gross and John Edward Hardy. Chicago: University of Chicago Press, 1966.

Carter, Paul. *Waldo Frank*. New York: Twayne Publishers, 1967.

Cash, W.J. *The Mind of the South*. New York: Alfred A. Knopf, 1941.

Clark, Kenneth. *The Gothic Revival*. New York: Humanities Press, 1970.

Cleaver, Eldridge. *Soul on Ice*. New York: McGraw-Hill Book Co., 1967.

Crane, Stephen. *The Red Badge of Courage and Selected Prose and Poetry*. New York: Holt, Rinehart & Winston, 1950.

Cruse, Harold. *The Crisis of the Negro Intellectual*. New York: Morrow, 1967.

cummings, e. e. *The Enormous Room*. New York: Modern Library, 1934.

Davis, William T., ed. *History of the Plymouth Plantation, 1606-1646*. New York: Gossett, 1908.

Dixon, Thomas. *The Clansman*. New York: Doubleday & Co., 1903.

DuBois, W. E. B. *The Souls of Black Folk: Essays and Sketches*. Chicago: McClurg, 1953.

Ellison, Ralph. *Invisible Man*. New York: Random House, 1947.

_____. *Shadow and Act.* New York: Random House, 1953.

Engle, Edwin A. *The Haunted Heroes of Eugene O'Neill.* Cambridge, Mass.: Harvard University Press, 1953.

Evans, Bertrand. *Gothic Drama from Walpole to Shelley.* Berkeley, Calif.: University of California Press, 1947.

Faulkner, William. *Absalom, Absalom!* New York: The Modern Library, 1951.

_____. *Go Down, Moses and Other Stories.* New York: Random House, 1942.

_____. *Intruder in the Dust.* New York: Random House, 1948.

_____. "Red Leaves," *These 13.* New York: Cape and Smith, 1931.

_____. *Requiem for a Nun.* New York: Random House, 1951.

_____. *Sartoris.* New York: Harcourt, Brace, 1929.

_____. *The Sound and the Fury.* New York: Random House, 1929.

Fiedler, Leslie A. *Love and Death in the American Novel.* New York: Stein and Day, 1967.

_____. *Waiting for the End.* New York: Stein and Day, 1965.

Frank, Waldo. *Holiday.* New York: Boni and Liverwright, 1923.

Frank, Waldo. *In the American Jungle.* New York: Farrar and Rinehart, 1937.

Frank, Waldo. *Our America.* New York: Boni and Liveright, 1919.

Franklin, John Hope. *From Slavery to Freedom: A History of American Negroes.* New York: Alfred A. Knopf, 1947.

Freud, Sigmund. *Civilization and its Discontents.* Translated by James Strachey. New York: W. W. Norton & Co., 1961.

Gaither, Francis. *The Red Cock Crows.* New York: Macmillan Co., 1944.

Gass, William, *Fiction and the Figures of Life,* New York: Vintage Books, 1959.

Gassner, John. "The Nature of O'Neill's Achievement: A Summary and Appraisal." In *O'Neill,* edited by John Gassner. Englewood Cliffs, N.J.: Prentice-Hall, 1964.

Gelb, Arthur and Gelb, Barbara. *O'Neill.* New York: Harper & Row, 1965.

Gibson, Donald. *The Fiction of Stephen Crane.* Carbondale, Ill.: Southern Illinois University Press, 1968.

Gloster, Hugh M. *Negro Voices in American Fiction*. Chapel Hill, N.C.: University of North Carolina Press, 1948.

Gossett, Louise. *Violence in Recent Southern Fiction*. Durham, N.C.: Duke University Press, 1965.

Gross, Seymour and John Edward Hardy, eds. *Images of the Negro in American Literature*. Chicago: University of Chicago Press, 1966.

Gullason, Thomas A. "The Symbolic Unity of *the Monster.*" *Modern Language Notes* 75 (1960): 660-68.

Gwynn, Frederick L., and Joseph L. Blotner, eds. *Faulkner in the University: Class Conferences at the University of Virginia.* Charlottesville, Va.: University of Virginia Press, 1959.

Hardy, John Edward. "Eudora Welty's Negroes." In *Images of the Negro in American Literature,* edited by Seymour L. Gross and John Edward Hardy. Chicago: University of Chicago Press, 1966.

Harris, Joel Chandler. *Free Joe and Other Georgian Sketches.* New York: P.F. Collier, 1887.

Heyward, DuBose. *The Half Pint Flask.* New York: Literary Guild, 1929.

————. *Mamba's Daughters.* New York: Literary Guild, 1929.

————. *Porgy.* New York: George H. Doran, 1925.

Hill, Herbert, ed. *Anger and Beyond: The Negro Writer in the United States.* New York: Viking Press, 1949.

Hoffman, Frederick. *The Twenties: American Writing in the Postwar Decade.* New York: Viking Press, 1955.

Howe, Irving. *William Faulkner: A Critical Study.* New York: Random House, 1951.

Hughes, Langston. *The Big Sea.* New York: Alfred A. Knopf, 1940.

Isaacs, Neil. "Life for Phoenix." *Sewanee Review* 71 (1963): 75-81.

Jones, LeRoi (Imamu Baraka). *Dutchman and the Slave.* New York: William Morrow & Co., 1964.

Jones, William. "Welty's 'A Worn Path.' " *Explicator* 15 (June 1957): Item 57.

Kahn, Sy. "Stephen Crane and the Giant Voices of the Night: An Explication of 'The Monster.' " In *Essays in Modern American Literature,* edited by Richard Langford. DeLand, Fla.: Everett-Edwards, 1963.

Kaplan, Sidney. "Herman Melville and the American National Sin: The Meaning of *Benito Cereno.*" *Journal of Negro History* 41 (1956): 311-38; 17 (1957): 11-37.

———. "Introduction." *The Narrative of Arthur Gordon Pym.* New York: Hill and Wang, 1960.

Klinkowitz, Jerome and John Somer, eds. *The Vonnegut Statement.* New York: Delacorte Press, 1973.

Klotz, Marvin. "Procrustian Revision in Faulkner's *Go Down, Moses.*" *American Literature* 36 (March 1965): 1-16.

Leeds, Barry. *The Structured Vision of Norman Mailer.* New York: New York University Press, 1969.

Locke, Alain, ed. *The New Negro: An Interpretation.* New York: Boni and Liveright, 1925.

Lovejoy, Arthur O., et al. *A Documentary History of Primitivism and Other Related Ideas.* Baltimore, Md.: Johns Hopkins Press, 1935.

Lowell, Robert. *The Old Glory,* New York: Farrar, Straus & Giroux, 1964.

McKay, Claude, *A Long Way from Home.* New York: L. Furman, 1937.

Mailer, Norman. *Advertisements for Myself.* New York: G. P. Putnam's Sons , 1959.

———. *An American Dream.* New York: Dial Press, 1965.

———. *The Fight.* Boston: Little, Brown & Co. 1975.

———. *The White Negro.* San Francisco: City Lights Books, 1958.

———. *Why Are We in Vietnam?* New York: G. P. Putnam's Sons, 1967.

Marx, Leo. *The Machine in the Garden.* New York: Oxford University Press, 1967.

Mather, Cotton. *The Negro Christianized.* Boston, 1706.

Melville, Herman. *Benito Cereno.* New York: Hayden, 1969.

Mayer, Charles. "Social Forms vs Human Brotherhood in Crane's *The Monster.*" *Ball State University Forum* 14 (Summer 1973): 30 – 36.

Moor, George. *Notes on the History of Slavery in Massachusetts.* New York: Negro Universities Press, 1968.

Nilon, Charles. *Faulkner and the Negro.* New York: Citadel Press, 1965.

O'Connor, William Van. "The Wilderness Theme in Faulkner's 'The Bear.' " *Accent* 13 (Winter 1953): 12-20.

O'Neill, Eugene. "All God's Chillun Got Wings." In *Nine Plays by Eugene O'Neill.* New York: Liveright, 1932.

――――. *The Emperor Jones.* New York: Appleton, 1921.

Page, Thomas Nelson. *In Old Virginia or Marse Chan and Other Stories.* New York: Charles Scribner's Sons, 1892.

Pearce, Roy Harvey. *The Savages of America: A Study of the Indian and the Idea of Civilization.* Baltimore, Md.: Johns Hopkins University Press, 1965.

Peterkin, Julia. *Scarlet Sister Mary.* Indianapolis, Ind.: Bobbs-Merrill, 1928.

Poe, Edgar Allan. *Complete Works of Edgar Allan Poe.* Edited by James A. Harrison. New York: G. D. Sproul, 1902.

Purkey, Raymond. *Vachel Lindsay: 1879-1931.* Paris: Nizet, 1968.

Ruggles, Eleanor. *The West-Going Heart: A Life of Vachel Lindsay.* New York: W. W. Norton & Co., 1959.

Russell, Irwin. "Christmas Night in the Quarters," *Collected Poems.* New York: Century, 1888.

Saffin, John. "The Negro's Character." In *Notes on the History of Slavery in Massachusetts,* edited by George Moore. New York, 1866.

Solataroff, Robert. *Down Mailer's Way.* Urbana, Ill.: University of Illinois Press, 1974.

Stallman, Robert W. *Stephen Crane.* New York: Braziller, 1968.

Strachey, William. "A true reportory of the wracke, and redemption of Sir Thomas Gates Knight; upon, and from the Ilands of the Bermudas . . ." *In Hakluytus Posthumus, or Parches His Pilgrimes,* edited by Samuel Purchas, vol. 19. Glasgow: MacLehose, 1906.

Tanner, Tony. *City of Words.* London: Jonathan Cape, 1971.

Thompson, Lawrence. "Mirror Analogues in *The Sound and the Fury.*" In *Faulkner: A Collection of Critical Essays,* edited by Frederick J. Hoffman and Olga W. Vickery. New York: Harcourt, Brace, 1963.

Thoreau, Henry David. *A Week on the Concord and Merrimack Rivers.* New York: Holt, Rinehart & Winston, 1963.

Tischler, Nancy M. *Black Masks: Negro Characters in Modern Southern Fiction.* University Park, Pa.: Pennsylvania State University Press, 1969.

Trachtenberg, Alan, ed. *Memoirs of Waldo Frank.* Amherst, Mass.: University of Massachusetts Press, 1973.

Turner, Darwin. *In a Minor Chord.* Carbondale, Ill.: Southern Illinois University Press, 1971.

Van Vechten, Carl. *Nigger Heaven.* New York: Grossett and Dunlap, 1926.

Volpe, Edmund. *A Reader's Guide to William Faulkner.* New York: Farrar, Strauss, 1964.

Vonnegut, Kurt, Jr. *Between Time and Timbuktu.* New York: Delacorte Press, 1972.

———. *Cat's Cradle.* New York: Delacorte Press, 1965.

———. *Sirens of Titan.* New York: Delacorte Press, 1959.

Waith, Eugene M. "Eugene O'Neill: An Exercise in Unmasking." In *O'Neill,* edited by John Gassner. Englewood Cliffs, N.J.: Prentice-Hall, 1964.

Welty, Eudora. *Selected Stories of Eudora Welty.* New York: Modern Library, 1936.

Wheeler, Otis B. "Faulkner's Wilderness." *American Literature* 31 (May 1959): 127-36.

Whitney, Lois. *Primitivism and the Idea of Progress in English Popular Literature of the Eighteenth Century.* Baltimore, Md.: Johns Hopkins University Press, 1934.

Williams, David. *Faulkner's Women.* Montreal: McGill-Queen's University Press, 1977.

Williams, Tennessee. *Sweet Bird of Youth.* New York: New Directions, 1959.

Wright, Richard. *Native Sons.* New York: Harper & Row, 1940.

Index